THEMES IN THE GOSPEL OF JOHN

Other Books by E. Edward Zinke

The Certainty of the Second Coming
(with Roland R. Hegstad)

THEMES IN THE GOSPEL OF JOHN

E. Edward Zinke
with John Reeve, Bill Knott,
Kiersten Zinke, Jiří Moskala,
and Anthony Kent

Nampa, Idaho | www.pacificpress.com

Cover design by Brandon Reese
Cover design resources: Lars Justinen

The authors assume full responsibility for the accuracy of all facts and quotations as cited in this book.

To order additional copies of this book, call 1-800-765-6955,
or visit AdventistBookCenter.com

ISBN 978-0-8163-7028-3

September 2024

Dedication

This book is dedicated to our amazing and talented grand-children: Kiersten, Jordan, Cameron, Ethan, Spencer, Aiden, Madison, and Marissa.

Contents

Foreword

I was raised in an environment that was founded on empiricism (learning from experience and observation) and rationalism (reason and logic over emotion and religion). The systems were never defined specifically, but they were implicit in the culture of the day.

These systems were part of the air that we breathed. They were essential to our education, our fellowship, and our relationship with God. God would surely act according to the principles of life that were extracted from the natural world. God would certainly abide by the universal principles of the universe—love, freedom, fairness, justice, reason, and so forth.

It was within this climate that I read the story of Nicodemus and his encounter with Jesus. At first, I had difficulty making sense of Jesus' abrupt response to the rabbi. It seemed impolite and mistaken. To me, Nicodemus was operating according to the basic principles of the universe. He should be appreciated for complimenting Jesus on His miracle-making ability. I explored it further in the chapter on Nicodemus in *The Desire of Ages*, but what I found there always perplexed me. My empirical-rational perspective balked each time I read it.

Its meaning was obscure until I read Ephesians 2:8 ("Faith . . . is the gift of God") and Hebrews 11:1 ("Faith is the substance of things hoped for, the evidence of things not seen"). This new perspective opened up an unexpected world. It added a new dimension to the study of Scripture, including the Gospel of John. It led me to a real conversion—a conversion of my heart as well as my mind.

From this new vantage point, I have reflected on the fourth gospel and many individuals have helped me write this book. I thank Ann, my wife, for her careful and supportive work. Gary Swanson spent tireless hours editing and pulling together the necessary parts. John Reeve wrote chapter 3, Bill Knott wrote chapter 8 and parts of chapter 10, Jiří Moskala wrote chapter 11, and Anthony Kent wrote chapters 12 and 13. I am grateful to each one.

May the Gospel of John lead us to a closer walk with Christ. Let us vow to meet at that great heavenly reunion—and may that be very soon!

E. Edward Zinke

Introduction

I was standing in front of a magnificent scene in the Swiss Alps. Fluffy clouds floated above roaring waterfalls. Rushing streams coursed through the valleys between mountainsides covered by a dense forest of pine trees. Nestled in the valley was a beautiful turquoise lake that reflected the sky.

A couple was eating lunch by a rushing stream at the outlet of the lake. Their young children were playing in and around some giant rocks, giggling as they chased their two dogs round and round the moss-covered boulders.

I was, in fact, standing before a painting. I could have zeroed in on the finer points of the artwork: the type of paintbrushes used to lay down the paint, the properties of the paint, or the canvas upon which the artist placed the paint. There were so many details that made the painting exquisite.

But in focusing on the minutiae, I would have overlooked the bigger picture! I would have missed the arresting elements that gave the painting its incredible beauty—the sky reflected in the lake, the snowcapped mountains, the deep-green forest complemented by the moss on the boulders, and the family enjoying lunch by the stream. These features combined to display the grandeur and beauty of that scene in the Alps.

The same challenge confronts us when we study the Bible. The particulars are important, but one needs to step back and grasp the grand themes in order to understand the message of Scripture. If we become buried in the details of exegesis, important as it is, we can miss the broad message of the passage.

In our study of the Gospel of John, we will mind the details because they are important. But we will also zero in on the grand themes, seeking to appreciate the beautiful tapestry of the gospel story. We will discover that the signs and miracles lead to testimonies, and the testimonies lead to a better understanding of Jesus.

John wants us to get better acquainted with Christ, for in Him is life. This life involves a relationship with the only true and eternal God. As our Creator, He longs to fellowship with us throughout eternity.

Just as the painting in the gallery transported me to the scenic mountains of Switzerland, I pray that the Gospel of John will carry us to the feet of Jesus, the Master Teacher. He invites us to listen, learn, and dwell with Him forever!

1

Signs That Point the Way

E. Edward Zinke

To best understand the message of a book, we must first understand its theme. For example, in the book of Hosea, the theme is God's intense love for His people. The book portrays that love in Hosea's relationship with his wife, Gomer. Hosea married her—a woman of ill repute—and not surprisingly, she broke their relationship by going after other men. Time and again, he wooed her back to himself.

Their relationship illustrated the Israelites' relationship with God. He had called the Israelites to a close relationship with Himself, and the Israelites responded by breaking the covenant again and again. Yet God was always there, offering forgiveness and restoration.

The theme of God's plan and care for His people is introduced in the book of Genesis through the story of Joseph, who experienced adversity at his brothers' hands. When Joseph later encountered them in his Egyptian court, he actually comforted them. By that time, Joseph had become powerful, second only to the pharaoh himself. We might expect Joseph to be vindictive and bitter, yet he said to his brothers, "Do not therefore be grieved or angry with yourselves because you sold me here; for God sent me before you to preserve life" (Genesis 45:5). In this moving moment of self-reflection, Joseph reiterated a principle of God's love for His people. God was in control in each instance of peril.

When sin entered the world, God announced a plan of salvation that He had established even before the beginning. The Bible says that God "chose us in Him [Jesus] before the foundation of the world, that we should be holy and without blame before Him in love" (Ephesians 1:4).

When sin pervaded the world, God was in control and sent a flood.

> The LORD saw that the wickedness of man was great in the earth, and that every intent of the thoughts of his heart was only evil continually. . . .
>
> The earth also was corrupt before God, and the earth was filled with violence (Genesis 6:5, 11).

When Abram went to Egypt, God protected his wife, Sarai. As an alien in that culture, Abram feared for his own safety because of his wife's beauty. He told the pharaoh that she was, in fact, his sister. As he might have anticipated, the pharaoh brought Sarai into his household, intending to take her as a wife. "But the LORD plagued Pharaoh and his house with great plagues because of Sarai" (Genesis 12:17). And the pharaoh angrily expelled Abram and Sarai from Egypt.

When the coming destruction of Sodom and Gomorrah threatened Abram's nephew Lot, God delivered Lot and his family.

The Son of God

These Old Testament themes are picked up in the New Testament but with a twist—the Messiah has arrived. He is the loving and caring God made human, and John aims to make this clear. "Truly Jesus did many other signs in the presence of His disciples, which are not written in this book; but these are written that you may believe that Jesus is the Christ, the Son of God, and that believing you may have life in His name" (John 20:30, 31).

John tells us exactly why he wrote his Gospel: so that we might believe that Jesus is the Christ, the Son of God, and that by believing, we might have life in His name! John tells us that he could have recorded many more signs or miracles, but he chose these specifically because they point to Jesus as the Christ, the Son of God, through whom we might receive eternal life.

It is important to note that John did not choose to report a miracle to prove the authenticity of Jesus' miracles. He chose to report it because of the character of the miraculous work—because it pointed to Jesus as the fulfillment of the Old Testament promise of the coming Messiah.

Water to wine

The first sign or miracle recorded in the Gospel of John took place early in the ministry of Christ. Jesus attended a wedding in Cana of Galilee (John 2:1–10), and during the course of the celebration, the wedding party ran out of grape juice.[1] Ceremonial water pots used for ritual purification were nearby, and Jesus asked the servants to fill them with water.

When the servants presented the water—now turned to juice—to the master of the feast, he was surprised. He observed that it was customary to serve the good juice first and then, when the guests had drunk well, to serve the inferior juice. But the best had been saved until last.

John is not simply narrating a story; he is showing how the miracle identified Jesus as the Messiah. For those who asked, "Why has the Messiah taken so long to come?" John can say, "The best is saved for last!"

Moses, a forerunner of the Messiah, also performed miracles when he arrived to lead Israel out of Egypt. After meeting God at the burning bush, he later went on to change the Nile River to blood (Exodus 7:14–22). He then led Israel through the Red Sea. Toward the end of his ministry, he prophesied that God would raise up a Prophet like him (see Deuteronomy 18:15–19).

When Jesus turned water into wine, Moses' prophecy was fulfilled. And what was the result? "This beginning of signs Jesus did in Cana of Galilee, and manifested His glory; and His disciples believed in Him" (John 2:11).

The next referenced miracle also took place in Cana. Jesus healed a nobleman's son with just a word, without even traveling to Capernaum, where the son was (John 4:46–54).

Imagine John holding a red pen so that he could underline the common themes of the miracles of the wedding wine and the nobleman's son.

1. Both miracles were signs (John 2:11; 4:48, 54).
2. Both took place in Cana of Galilee (John 2:1, 11; 4:46, 54).
3. Both elicited faith (John 2:11; 4:50, 53).

This response of faith fulfilled the purpose for which John was writing his book. "These are written that you may believe that Jesus is the Christ, the Son of God, and that believing you may have life in His name" (John 20:31).

The pool of Bethesda

The next sign seems simple. Jesus walked by the pool of Bethesda. It was crowded with chronically ill people who waited at the water's edge, hoping to be the first to enter it if the waters were stirred. People thought that such a person would be healed.

Jesus walked by, saw a disabled man, and asked whether he wanted to be healed. The man answered that he had no one to assist him into the waters when they were moved. Jesus said, "Take up your bed and walk" (John 5:8). The man took up his bed and walked.

Straightforward and simple? No! Not so simple! Jesus made what appears to be a strategic mistake.

One would think the crowd should be celebrating. The man was healed—no more long years of waiting by the pool. But this healing presented a major problem to the elders. It took place on the Sabbath, and for them, this required litigation and judgment for breaking the Sabbath.

Healing was not legal on the Sabbath unless there was an emergency. The man had been disabled for thirty-eight years. There was no way to slip by the courts on this one. If the problem had been some malady of the brain, the incident might squeak by. But this man was fine except for his legs, and this did not qualify for a Sabbath exception.

So, John finds that this is an excellent opportunity to define Christ's pedigree. It takes only nine verses to describe the situation. But then John takes more than thirty verses to evangelize—to tell the story of Jesus. This provides him with the opportunity to showcase Jesus' assertion that He is the Son of God, equal to and one with the Father!

After the healing, the leaders asked the man who had healed him and told him to take up his bed and walk. After all, it was the Sabbath! No one had the authority to give that kind of permission.

But the healed man did not know who had made him well. What an opportunity for John: *I am writing my Gospel so that Jesus will be known!*

When the man who had been healed bumped into Jesus in the temple, Jesus revealed Himself as the person who made him well. The man went to tell the rulers that Jesus was his Healer. Therefore, the leaders "sought all the more to kill" Jesus on two accounts: (1) He broke the Sabbath; and (2) He "said that God was His Father, making Himself equal with God" (verse 18).

In verses 19 and 20, Jesus explained that the Father and the Son work in unison, and as a result, the Father will show greater works that the rulers may marvel. Notice that John continues the theme of the signs. John says that we have just begun!

Both God the Father and God the Son have the power of resurrection (verse 21). They work in harmony with each other. From God's perspective, there is a time coming when those who hear the words of Christ will come forth from the grave.

Witnesses

Moving from miracle accounts, John now turns to witnesses. The first one is John the Baptist. He testified to the truth and testified to the messiahship of Christ, and the leaders listened to John the Baptist for a while (verses 31–35).

In addition to the witness of John the Baptist, Christ's works bore witness that God had sent Him (verse 36). His Father, whom the rulers had rejected, also bore witness to Him (verses 37, 38). And the Scriptures, which the leaders treasured, testified of Him (verses 39, 40).

Finally, Jesus cites the witness of Moses, the revered leader who had brought the Israelites out of Egypt. "If you believed Moses, you would believe Me; for he wrote about Me. But if you do not believe his writings, how will you believe My words?" (verses 46, 47). Jesus could not have made it any clearer. In rejecting the testimony of Moses, the rulers were rejecting the prophesied Messiah. This stinging reproof was Christ's all-out attempt to get His listeners' attention and win their hearts to His claims.

---

1. In *The Desire of Ages*, Ellen G. White states that the juice was non-alcoholic. *The Desire of Ages* (Mountain View, CA: Pacific Press®, 1940), 149.

2

Signs of Divinity

E. Edward Zinke

After healing the man who had been disabled for thirty-eight years, Jesus crossed the Sea of Galilee, and a large multitude followed Him. It was the time of Passover—the commemoration of Israel's exodus from Egypt—and Jesus used this moment to link Himself with Moses, the great deliverer of the Old Testament. Continuing to a hillside, Jesus taught the people all day long (Matthew 14:13–21), and as the end of the day approached, He knew the large multitude would need food.

So Jesus turned to Philip and asked where they might buy bread. Then Andrew, another disciple, who overheard this conversation, pointed to a lad who had brought his own lunch of five barley loves and two fish. It was pitifully inadequate to feed a few people, let alone the crowd of more than five thousand. Nevertheless, Jesus asked them to sit on the grassy slope.

Jesus gave thanks and began to break the bread and the fish. The disciples took the food and started distributing it to the crowd. This little lad's lunch continued to multiply until everyone was fed. And twelve baskets of leftovers were collected!

Then the men, who had seen the signs that Jesus did, said, "This is truly the Prophet who is to come into the world" (John 6:14). But they were looking not only for a prophet but also for a king. Imagine a king who could perform miracles, lead their armies, and deliver them from the Romans! In times of war, food is a scarce resource, and healing injured warriors is a high priority. Unfortunately, their hopes for a king did not coincide with God's plan for a Messiah. Jesus perceived that they were about to take Him by acclamation and make Him king and, soon after, left for the other side of the lake to avoid them.

One of the themes of the Gospel of John is that Jesus knows human thought and intent. This is illustrated in the conversation with the crowd when they caught up with Jesus the next day. Recognizing their objective, He took control of the conversation, saying, "Do not labor for the food which perishes, but for the food which endures to everlasting life, which the Son of Man will give you, because God the Father has set His seal on Him" (verse 27).

The crowd asked how they could do the works of God. Jesus answered, "This is the work of God, that you believe in Him whom He sent" (verse 29).

The crowd then asked, "What sign will You perform then, that we may see it and believe You? What work will You do? Our fathers ate the manna in the desert; as it is written, 'He gave them bread from heaven to eat' " (verses 30, 31).

Imagine! Jesus had just fed the five thousand the day before, and now they asked for a sign that they might believe! The lesson is inescapable: we believe, and then we see the miracles. Faith is not based upon empirical verification. We see miracles when we come with eyes of faith. This miracle of feeding the five thousand helps John make the case that Jesus, the humble carpenter, is indeed the promised Messiah.

The man blind from birth

The next sign of divinity is found in John 9. As Jesus and His disciples were walking one day, they passed a man who had been blind from birth. This raised a serious question in the disciples' minds. Who sinned—this man or his parents? Four possibilities are mentioned in the story.

The disciples thought that either the blind man or his parents had sinned (verse 2). The Pharisees thought that Jesus was the sinner (verse 24). And Jesus declared that the Pharisees were the sinners because of their spiritual blindness in rejecting Him (verses 40, 41).

Taking pity on the blind man, Jesus put clay on his eyes and told him to wash in the pool of Siloam. The man was healed, and the works of God were revealed in this miracle. Yet Jesus did not meet the expectations for the Messiah because He performed this miracle on the Sabbath day.

This Sabbath healing caused no small stir. Much effort was put forth to discover whether the man who was healed had really been born blind and, if he had been, who healed him. And where was the Person who had healed him? The Healer surely could not be from God because He healed on the Sabbath. But some of the Pharisees said He could not do such things if He were *not* of God.

Endeavoring to get answers to their questions, the Pharisees decided to ask the healed man's parents if he had been born blind. His parents confirmed that he was blind at birth, but as to how he was healed, they did not know.

The Pharisees returned to the man for details about his healing. They asked what he claimed his Healer had done to bring him his sight. He answered them curtly, reminding them that they had asked him about this earlier. Why were they asking follow-up questions? The healed man then asked, using irony and some quick wit, if the Pharisees were also thinking of becoming disciples of this Healer.

The Pharisees answered sarcastically that the man might be a disciple of Jesus, but they were disciples of Moses—meaning followers of the laws and traditions established since Moses' time. They reminded him that God had spoken to Moses, but they were uncertain where the authority of this new Healer came from.

The healed man's answer was in the same tone: How could the authority of someone who had performed such a miracle be in question? Surely, if someone could heal a person of blindness, it must be the result of the healer's relationship with God.

The Pharisees were aghast. How could this untaught man presume to question their authority?

Sometime later, Jesus encountered the healed man again, although the man did not recognize Him as his Healer at first. Jesus asked him if he believed in the Son of God, and the man responded that he would believe if he ever encountered the Son of God.

At this moment, Jesus identified Himself to the man born blind as his Healer—and as the Son of God.

And the man declared, "I believe!"

Jesus said sorrowfully that there were others who were blind to His claim to be the Son of God.

Recounting this sign of the healing of the blind man gives John the opportunity to tell us who Jesus is. He is the One who can overcome blindness.

The theme of signs in John 9 intersects with several other themes in the Gospel of John. In this miracle, John reaffirms that Jesus is the I AM—the Light of the world (verse 5). He also deals with Jesus' mysterious origin: Who is He? Where is He from? What is His mission? (verses 12, 29). The figure of Moses, mentioned in previous miracle accounts, is again referenced by the Pharisees in the healing of the blind man (verses 28, 29). There is also the theme of the response of Christ's listeners. Some loved darkness rather than light, while others responded in faith (verses 16–18, 35–41).

The resurrection of Lazarus

The feeding of the five thousand and the healing of the blind man were tremendous miracles, but apart from the resurrection of Christ, the resurrection of Lazarus was the crowning sign of the divinity of Christ. This miracle also highlighted the divide that ensued; some believed in Christ, while many others doubted. Even as the resurrection of Lazarus unfolded, the doubters began to plan Christ's death.

Note the similarities between the raising of Lazarus and the healing of the blind man. Both the man's blindness and Lazarus's sickness were allowed so that the glory of God would be revealed through their healing. It is the language in the three verses that links the two miracles: In the case of the blind man, "Neither this man nor his parents sinned, but that the *works of God should be revealed* in him" (John 9:3; emphasis added). And Jesus had this to say about Lazarus. "This sickness is not unto death, but *for the glory of God, that the Son of God may be glorified* through it" (John 11:4; emphasis added). (Verse 40 echoes verse 4.) Both miracles revealed the glory of God (John 9:3; 11:4, 40).

Word came to Christ and the disciples that Lazarus was seriously sick and possibly near death. Instead of going to Lazarus immediately, Jesus delayed His departure for two days. The disciples were surprised, first, that Jesus did not leave at once, and second, that He decided to go two days later. Such a journey was dangerous, for the authorities sought to kill

Jesus. Why take the risk of this dangerous journey if Lazarus's condition was not serious? But Jesus explained that He would be protected because His time to die had not yet come—a theme familiar in the rest of the Gospel of John (John 11:9, 10; cf. John 9:4; 12:35; 17:4).

While Jesus tarried, Lazarus died. When Jesus arrived in Bethany, Lazarus's sister Martha went out to meet Him. She expressed her questions and doubts and affirmed her faith in the resurrection. "Lord, if You had been here, my brother would not have died. But even now I know that whatever You ask of God, God will give You" (John 11:21, 22). Martha's declaration of faith in the resurrection and in Christ, the Savior of the world, is another confirming testimony in the Gospel of John.

Lazarus's other sister, Mary, was attended by many mourners; some of them had come from Jerusalem upon hearing of the death of Lazarus. These mourners had doubts in their minds: *If Jesus can open the eyes of the blind, could He not have prevented this man—a close personal friend—from dying?*

Arriving at Lazarus's tomb, Jesus asked that the stone be removed. Concern was raised that the body stank after four days. This is an important point. This fact needed to be noted in order to verify that the resurrection was not a stunt! Lazarus was truly dead. And he really was resurrected.

John chose to include this miracle in his Gospel because it pointed to Jesus as the Life-Giver. The miracle took place for the glory of God and the glory of His Son (verse 4). It was strong support for John's theme that Jesus is the Son of God and that by believing, we might have life through Him (John 20:30, 31).

The feeding of the five thousand, the healing of the man born blind, and the resurrection of Lazarus generated two basic responses. Some believed in Christ as the Savior of the world, and others used these events as reasons to plan for His execution on the cross. The evidence was clear, but hardened hearts refused to believe.

The same evidence confronts us today. The Gospel of John poses the most important questions we will ever ponder. Will we stand with Jesus? Or will we stand against Him? Let us stand together on the side of our Savior.

3

The Backstory: The Prologue

John Reeve

The prologue to the Gospel of John—John 1:1–18—begins and ends with a description of the divine nature of the Word as Creator God in relation to God. The rest of the prologue describes the Word as a human in this world, specifically identifying the Word as Jesus Christ (verse 17). As such, it is a fitting beginning to a book with the stated goal of leading the reader to believe that Jesus is the Messiah, the Son of God, and that by believing in Him, one "may have life" (John 20:31).

John first introduces the eternal Word as the fully divine Creator (John 1:1–3) before continuing with this same Word becoming flesh and dwelling among us (verse 14). Most of the book is devoted to showing the Word acting and interacting in flesh: performing the signs, revealing the love and sovereignty of God to us, going through the Passion and on to the cross as our Savior, and in the finale, assuring and empowering His disciples, then and now, to bear witness to His actions for us and His interactions with us.

How should we think about Logos?

The first question that faces us is, What does John intend by using the term *Logos* (Word) to identify the coming Savior? He could have used many other terms and did use many other terms: God, Light, life, Jesus Christ, and *monogenes* (unique, one and only, only son). Instead of leading with any of these other terms for our Savior, he starts with *Logos*. We will begin answering this question by briefly reviewing the semantic range of the term *logos* in the first-century Greco-Roman world.

The term *logos* could designate a written word or a phrase—or even a treatise or whole book. It could be used to refer to a spoken word, phrase, or lecture. When used in the plural, it could represent a set of doctrines or beliefs. It could represent a law or set of laws. It could also refer to thinking (as in logical thought) and, by extension, the location of human thought.

The first-century Greco-Roman world had an extremely broad semantic range for the term *logos*. Heraclitus of Ephesus, writing in the fifth century before Christ, emphasized that law, or principle, was ensured in the universe by a divine power he called logos. While Plato had much to say about logos, which will be covered below, it is the Stoics who had the broadest conceptualization of the word. In Stoic thought, as represented in the writings of Chrysippus, logos had four major nuances in regard to the world and creation. First, logos was used to identify the idea of the created world in the mind of God; second, it designated the creating power who emanated from God in order to do the actual fabricating of the created world. Third, logos was also used to denote the whole of the created, material world. Fourth, it was used to describe that which enabled humans to perceive the powers and the principles within the universe and beyond.

Before introducing more philosophical concepts of logos,

it is important to address a hermeneutical (principle of biblical interpretation) issue regarding John's relationship with philosophical terms and categories. The Bible does not need philosophy to be understood correctly, as is so often insisted on by medieval scholastics and even many modern interpreters. The Bible is its own interpreter, and the use of words within the Bible should be understood first as defined by the author using the word as framed within its context. We often use historical knowledge to understand the context, including knowledge of the philosophical commonalities within the temporal and cultural context into which the inspired Bible writer communicates the revealed message. History informs the contextual understanding but never dictates the categories of what is communicated. The Bible writer often corrects the understanding of his contemporaries with revealed truth.

Plato and Logos

For two thousand years, Christians have read John's prologue, often consciously using contemporary philosophical categories as the basis for interpretation. It behooves us then to know some philosophy, not so much to interpret the correct meaning of John's prologue but to protect us from unconsciously imbibing the tradition of reading John within the confines of the broad Platonic tradition of philosophy. As we shall see, John corrects Platonic thought rather than following it. The proper hermeneutic is to let John define what he means by Logos and contrast that with philosophical expectations.

More precise to the philosophical understanding that was most prominent in the first-century Greco-Roman world was the Middle Platonic view of Logos. Though largely using Stoic terminology, this view was primarily derived from Plato's dialogue titled *Timaeus*. Herein is one of Plato's most well-known descriptions of the creation of the material world (which probably encompasses what we now term the *universe*).

The basic picture is of a single God, whom Plato designates as *Monad*—the first numeral, the unit—because he is the first principle and is a simple power, undivided and uncontained. The Monad is completely transcendent, pure mind, pure spirit, entirely beyond, and incapable of any interaction with the material, sense-perceptible world in which we live. The Monad, as described by Plato, has no connection with and no direct relationship to our world or to us. He is all-powerful, good, and even beneficent but cannot be perceived as loving. Loving demands vulnerability, and the Monad has no vulnerabilities. In fact, the Monad could plan and design this world but could not actually create it because he is only transcendent. The Monad, therefore, emanated the *Dyad* from himself. This Dyad, or second, Plato also calls the Logos and the Demiurge. This second is different enough from the Monad to be able to have division abilities that allow him to be immanent as well as transcendent. The difference allows him to fabricate creation—the "hands-on" creator. The difference also allows him to interact with the created, material, and sense-perceptible world with which the simple Monad could not directly interact. In Plato's model, it is the difference between the Monad and the Dyad, or Logos, that allows the Logos to be in relationship with humans.

John's description of Logos

With all these options for the meaning of *Logos* in John 1, how do we limit the meaning of what John envisioned when he chose the designation *Logos*? We listen carefully to how John introduces the Logos: with God and as God. Before Creation, the Logos existed. He existed with God. He existed as God.

John's description stands on the shoulders of the philosophical use of Logos and corrects it.

In John 1:1, "with" denotes the togetherness of at least two beings with some sort of individuality. The Person John designates as "Logos" (Word) is not the same Person he designates as "Theos" (God) because he shows Them to be together. So far, this is in agreement with Plato's *Timaeus* as far as individuation is concerned, but John 1:1 does not indicate the Logos having a source in this pre-enfleshment state. This is a corrective on Plato. Plato's Logos came from, emanated from, the Monad. John has no emanation—no source for the Logos; He is presented as self-existent, which is the same as Theos. A bigger corrective on Plato's view of the Monad and the Logos is the next phrase: the Logos was Theos.

The Logos being Theos needs a simple explanation. At times in the New Testament, Theos refers to a Person who is God, such as Paul's use of Theos throughout his greetings and benedictions in his letters (e.g., God the Father in Romans 1:7–9). Paul also uses Theos for "our Savior" in Titus 1:3, 4. The New Testament also uses Theos as a descriptor of what a person is, his nature. In this case, John is describing the Logos as God, using *Theos* as a linking word, connecting it to *Logos*.

Thus, John expresses the full divinity of the Logos. He is God, opposing the Platonic understanding of the difference between the Monad and the Logos. For John, the Logos was God with the same nature as God the Father. (The full divinity of Christ can be found in many other scriptures, including Colossians 1:19; 2:9; Philippians 2:5–8; Hebrews 1:2, 3.)

Similarly, for Plato, the Monad could not create because he was pure intellect and simply One. The different and dividable Dyad, the Logos, could fabricate creation because he was different. But for John, it requires full divinity—actual God—to create. The very first phrase of the book of John reads like the very first phrase of the Bible: "In the beginning God . . ." (Genesis 1:1). Here in the Gospel of John, it reads, "In the beginning was the Word" (John 1:1). The informed reader of established Scripture cannot help but recognize the idea that this Word is in the position of God (Theos). As Moses does in Genesis, John equates creatorship with full divinity.

Eternal Creator and Companion

Our first question of what John means by his use of *Logos* as his primary designation of our Savior can be answered from his writing itself. The Logos was the eternal companion of God and was Himself eternally God, with no indicated beginning or source outside Himself. As the Eternal God, the Logos created. This is a major contrast to the Platonic view of God as the Monad and the Logos. For Plato, the Logos was neither God, with the same nature as the Monad God, nor was he self-existent without source. Plato's Logos emanated from the Monad, was different in nature from God, and was able to fabricate the created world because of this difference.

This brings us to our second biggest question in the prologue to the Gospel of John: Why did the Logos become flesh and dwell among us?

Before we investigate John's description of the Word's task on our planet, it must be acknowledged that for Plato, and the whole of the philosophic view of God, the idea of God becoming human is outrageous. Nothing could be further from philosophers' minds than God emptying (kenosis, as in Philippians 2:7) Himself and becoming human. There are all kinds of ways different philosophers perceived of humans having bits of divinity or becoming more divine, but for God to become human is a non sequitur. Yet that is the very corrective that

John gives in this introduction to Jesus Christ and His actions on our planet using the title *Logos*.

Following the establishment of the Logos as the eternal Creator and companion of God who is also fully God and the description of the creation (John 1:1–3), John first confirms the foundation of the relationship between the Logos and His creation as He joins it: Life and Light (verses 4, 5). These two themes are prominent and are often together, especially in the first half of John's Gospel.

Life

The theme of life in the Gospel of John is most often associated with eternal life, as found in this prologue and in John 3–6; 10–12; 17:

- In the story of Nicodemus in John 3, John asserts that believing in the Son leads to eternal life (verses 15, 16).
- With the woman at the well, the Living Water leads to eternal life (John 4:10, 14).
- In John 5, John reports that after healing the disabled man on the Sabbath, Jesus asserted that the Son, like the Father, gives life, and those who believe have eternal life (verses 21, 24).
- In John 6, on the day after feeding the five thousand, Jesus gives the assurance that He is the Bread of Life; those who eat of it have eternal life, and He will raise them up in the last day (verses 35, 40, 47, 51, 54, 58).
- In John 10, in the midst of His teaching, Jesus tells the people that He came that they may have life, and later in the teaching, He overtly states that "I give them eternal life" (verses 10, 28).
- And so it goes until John 17, when, in His final prayer

> for His disciples, Jesus says, "And this is eternal life, that they may know You, the only true God, and Jesus Christ whom You have sent" (verse 3).

This consistent association between life and eternal life throughout the Gospel leads the reader to assume that the life referred to in the purpose statement of the book in John 20:31 is intended to mean eternal life—that is, salvation.

Light

The theme of light is less dominant than life in the Gospel but still features in this prologue and in John 3; 5; 8; 9; 11; 12. Again, like the theme of life, light has more prominence in the first half of the book. Light is usually contrasted with darkness as it features in John, and light consistently expels darkness unless darkness is chosen over light.

Another significant feature of the theme of light in the Gospel of John is that it is present in the person of Jesus, who came to our world: "In Him was life, and the life was the light of men" (John 1:4); "the true Light . . . coming into the world" (verse 9); "the light has come into the world" (John 3:19); "I am the light of the world" (John 8:12); and preparing for His death, He said, "A little while longer the light is with you" (John 12:35).

Throughout these references to the theme of light, John suggests that the true Light is Jesus and the truth He brings about God and salvation. John 3:20, 21 hints at judgment in that all human deeds are within the sight of God, but John 12:36 has the invitation to "believe in the light, that you may become sons of light." This is a throwback to verses 9–13 in the prologue, in which the core of the reason for the Logos becoming flesh is revealed: to bring the true Light to every human (John 1:9) and that whoever receives Him He gives the right to become children of God and be born of God (verses 12, 13). This is what the theme of light points to—the truth, in the person of Christ, revealing the universal invitation to salvation.

Salvation

It is important to emphasize what John articulates in his Gospel about the nature of this salvation. Even here in the prologue, John goes out of his way to show the importance of John the Baptist as a witness to Christ and His salvation (John 1:6–8). John the Baptist was not the light but bore witness to the Light that all might believe (verses 8, 9). But what should we believe in or, rather, in whom? A few verses later comes the resounding answer: "Behold! The Lamb of God who takes away the sin of the world!" (verse 29). John makes it abundantly clear that Jesus Christ, the Logos, became flesh in order to die as the sacrifice for human sin (John 3:14; 12:32, 33).

So the joint themes of light and life work together to display the reason for the Logos to come to live among us as one of us in order to save us as the Lamb of God: "Whoever believes in Him should not perish but have everlasting life" (John 3:16). God has become a human in order to give salvation and truth—life and light.

Prevenient grace

The same section of the prologue that introduces salvation and truth through the themes of life and light also emphasizes the universality of the offer of salvation (John 1:6–13). In fact, these verses introduce all three of the major elements of prevenient grace[1]: it is initiated by God, offered to all, and empowered by God.

The first indication that God is initiating the offer of salvation, rather than waiting for humans to initiate contact with Him, comes in the form of sending John to bear witness to the One who has come to Earth as Life and Light. Through the Logos, Jesus, the true Light, *God initiates our salvation.*

Second, Jesus came to offer salvation to all humans. John the Baptist was sent so that "all . . . might believe" through the true Light (verse 7), and the true Light gives light to "everyone" (verse 9, NRSV). So, by the time we get to verse 12, "as many as received Him" is not meant as a limitation to a few but an offer to all. *God offers salvation to all.*

The third element of prevenient grace is also found in these verses: God empowers the choice to be saved and the rebirth of salvation. Verse 9 emphasizes that the true Light gives light before the choice in verse 12. So, the choice to receive Christ is empowered by His gift of light. The choice is followed by another gift from Christ: He gives power and authority to us to become children of God. On top of that, the rebirth is given by the will of God (verse 13). *God empowers every step of salvation.* All three major elements of prevenient grace are introduced by John in the prologue to his Gospel.

---

1. In simple terms, *prevenient grace* is the grace of God given to individuals that releases them from their bondage to sin and enables them to come to Christ in faith but does not guarantee that they will actually do so. "What Is Prevenient Grace?," Got Questions, last updated July 25, 2022, https://www.gotquestions.org/prevenient-grace.html.

4

Witnesses of Christ as the Messiah

E. Edward Zinke

"There was a man sent from God, whose name was John" (John 1:6). John the Baptist's mission was to bear witness to Jesus, who is the Light of the world. "He was not that Light, but was sent to bear witness of that Light" (verse 8). "John bore witness of Him and cried out, saying, 'This was He of whom I said, "He who comes after me is preferred before me, for He was before me" ' " (verse 15).

It was the Messianic era. The seventy weeks of Daniel's prophecy about the coming Messiah were nearing their close. It was almost time for the fulfillment of this prophecy and the coming of the Messiah. The Jews, however, expected the coming Messiah to be a king who would overthrow the Romans. But there had been previous riots caused by would-be kings, so it was important for the Jewish leaders to stay on top of the situation with John the Baptist. John the Baptist and his followers could upset the stability of the current political scene. The Jewish authorities did not want to lose favor with the Romans.

Though the Jews looked for the coming of a secular messiah, the goal of the Gospel of John was to change the common understanding of the Messiah so that people could recognize Jesus as the fulfillment of the prophecies regarding the coming king. The Messiah would not be an earthly ruler. The Messiah was coming to renew the relationship between the people and God—to bring salvation through faith in the One who was to come.

The One who was to come transforms the way we understand the world. The Gospel of John is not based upon the philosophy of the Greeks or the empiricism of the Jews but upon "Christ the power of God and the wisdom of God" (1 Corinthians 1:24). The knowledge that Jesus is the Christ comes from God Himself through the convicting power of the Holy Spirit.

The Jews sent a delegation of priests and Levites from Jerusalem to John the Baptist, who was baptizing near Bethany beyond the Jordan River, about twenty-five miles from Jerusalem. They came with an inquiry. They wanted to understand who John was and by what right he was baptizing.

They asked quite bluntly, "Who are you?" (John 1:19).

Already anticipating the purpose of their visit, John emphatically answered that he was not the Christ.

"Then who are you? Are you Elijah?" (verse 21, NIV).

He answered that he was not.

Then they asked, "Are you the Prophet?" (verse 21).

But John was not the Prophet either. He answered no.

The delegation from Jerusalem needed to know who John was. They could hardly return to Jerusalem without that knowledge. So they pressed again: Who are you? The Prophet? They were likely referring to Deuteronomy 18: "I will raise up for them a Prophet like you [Moses] from among their brethren, and will put My words in His mouth, and He shall speak to them all that I command Him" (verse 18). Notice the similarity to God's call to Moses: "You shall speak to him and put the words in his mouth" (Exodus 4:15).

So they asked again: "What do you say about yourself?" (John 1:22).

He answered, referring to the prophet Isaiah,

> "I am
>
> 'The voice of one crying in the wilderness:
> "Make straight the way of the LORD" ' " (verse 23).

So the next question was, "Why then do you baptize if you are not the Christ, nor Elijah, nor the Prophet?" (verse 24).

John answered, "I baptize with water, but there stands One among you whom you do not know" (verse 26).

"The next day John saw Jesus coming toward him, and said, 'Behold! The Lamb of God who takes away the sin of the world! This is He of whom I said, "After me comes a Man who is preferred before me, for He was before me." I did not know Him' " (verses 29–31).

This lack of knowledge of the Messiah is a theme in the Gospel of John. Time and again, it is not known who Jesus is. The purpose of the Gospel of John is to make Him known.

Andrew and Peter follow Christ

As John the Baptist was standing by the river, he testified that he saw the Spirit descending upon Jesus and remaining upon Him and that He is the One who baptizes with the Holy Spirit. "I have seen and testified that this is the Son of God" (verse 34).

The following day, John the Baptist was with two of his disciples, and as Jesus passed by, John said, "Behold the Lamb of God!" (verse 36). These disciples left John to spend the day with Jesus. "Moved by an irresistible impulse, they followed Jesus,—anxious to speak with Him, yet awed and silent, lost in the overwhelming significance of the thought, 'Is this the Messiah?' "[1] Desiring to be with Him, they spent the day with Him.

Their next desire was to share their experience with others. Andrew, one of the two disciples, immediately found his brother, Simon, and said, "We have found the Messiah" (verse 41). Andrew brought Simon to Jesus, and Jesus knew who he was, saying, " 'You are Simon the son of Jonah. You shall be called Cephas' (which is translated, A Stone)" (verse 42).

Here again, John highlights an important theme in the Gospel of John: Jesus knows what is inside a person's heart.

The witness of Philip and Nathanael

Next, Jesus went to Galilee and called Philip to follow Him. Philip was from Bethsaida, the same city as Andrew and Peter. Philip was anxious to share the message of the Messiah with Nathanael, who had also heard John the Baptist. Nathanael was moved by the message of John the Baptist and was studying Scripture to learn more about the promised Savior.[2] He was a devout student of the Torah and a committed Israelite.

Philip's declaration to Nathanael fits the overall emphasis of John's Gospel and mentions the name of Moses, which is often invoked in John's account. "Philip found Nathanael and said to him, 'We have found Him of whom Moses in the law, and also the prophets, wrote' " (verse 45; cf. John 1:17; 3:14; 6:32; 9:28, 29).

Nathanael raised a simple question that was right to the point: "Can anything good come out of Nazareth?" (John 1:46). Nathanael lived in Cana, which was a short distance from Nazareth. He may have been speaking from firsthand knowledge.

Philip gave a simple answer. He could have begun with philosophy, rationalism, empiricism, or one of the many other philosophies of his age. Instead, he simply invited Nathanael to come and see.

Jesus met Nathanael on the trail and said he was "an Israelite indeed" (verse 47).

Nathanael asked, "How do You know me?" (verse 48).

Jesus answered, "I saw you while you were still under the fig tree" (verse 48, NIV). (Some interpret this as a code for "a student of the Torah"—an Israelite indeed.)

John is beginning to weave the various themes—the signs of Jesus' divinity, His knowledge of what is in a person's heart, and the witnesses of who Jesus is—into one beautiful tapestry. And then Nathanael pulls it all together!

Nathanael cried out, "Rabbi, You are the Son of God! You are the King of Israel!" (verse 49).

Then Jesus offered this prophecy: "Most assuredly, I say to you, hereafter you shall see heaven open, and the angels of God ascending and descending upon the Son of Man" (verse 51).

As an author, John carefully records this conversation. *I will write it up so people clearly understand that their salvation is through Jesus Christ!*

Nicodemus

"Nicodemus held a high position of trust in the Jewish nation. He was highly educated, and possessed talents of no ordinary character, and he was an honored member of the national council. With others, he had been stirred by the teaching of Jesus. Though rich, learned, and honored, he had been strangely attracted by the humble Nazarene. The lessons that had fallen from the Saviour's lips had greatly impressed him, and he desired to learn more of these wonderful truths."[3]

The chapter in *The Desire of Ages* that records this account offers a deeper spiritual truth:

> Christ's use of His authority in cleansing the temple had ignited the hatred of the priests and rulers. They felt they should not tolerate such boldness from an obscure Galilean. But not all agreed about putting an end to His work. Some feared to oppose One whom the Spirit of God so evidently moved. They knew that the Jews were subjects of a heathen nation because they had stubbornly rejected God's reproofs. They feared that in plotting against Jesus the priests and rulers were following in the steps of their ancestors and would bring fresh disasters on the nation. Nicodemus shared these feelings. In the Sanhedrin, Nicodemus advised caution and moderation. He urged that if Jesus really carried authority from God, it would be dangerous to reject His warnings. The priests did not dare to ignore this counsel.
>
> Nicodemus had anxiously studied the prophecies relating to the Messiah. The more he searched, the stronger was his conviction that Jesus was the One who was to come. He had been distressed by how the priests had profaned the temple. He witnessed Jesus driving out the buyers and the sellers. He saw the Savior healing the sick, and he saw their looks of joy and heard their words of praise. He could not doubt that Jesus of Nazareth was the One sent from God. . . .

In Christ's presence, Nicodemus felt strangely timid, and he tried to conceal this. "Rabbi, we know that You are a teacher come from God; for no one can do these signs that You do unless God is with him." He chose his words to express and to invite confidence, but they really expressed unbelief. He did not acknowledge Jesus to be the Messiah, but only a teacher sent from God. . . .

Nicodemus had come to enter into a discussion, but Jesus laid open the foundation principles of truth. He said, "You don't need to have your curiosity satisfied, but to have a new heart. You must receive a new life from above before you can appreciate heavenly things. Until this change takes place, discussing My authority or My mission with Me will result in no saving good.". . .

Surprised out of his self-composure, he answered in words full of irony, "How can a man be born when he is old?" Like many others, he revealed that nothing in the natural heart responds to spiritual things. Spiritual things are spiritually discerned.

Raising His hand with quiet dignity, the Savior applied the truth even more closely and with greater assurance: "Most assuredly, I say to you, unless one is born of water and the Spirit, he cannot enter the kingdom of God." Nicodemus knew that Christ was referring to water baptism and the renewing of the heart by the Spirit of God. He was convinced that he was in the presence of the One whom John the Baptist had foretold. . . .

Jesus continued, "That which is born of the flesh is flesh, and that which is born of the Spirit is spirit." By nature the heart is evil. . . . The fountain of the heart must be purified before the stream can become pure. Those who try to reach heaven by their own works in keeping the law are attempting the impossible. The Christian's life is not a modification of the old but a transformation of nature, a death to self and sin, and a new life altogether. This change can come about only by the Holy Spirit.

Nicodemus was still perplexed, and Jesus used the wind to illustrate His meaning. "The wind blows where it wishes, and you hear the sound of it, but cannot tell where it comes from and where it goes. So is everyone who is born of the Spirit." . . .

Wind produces effects that we can see and feel. So the work of the Spirit on the heart will reveal itself in every act of the person who has felt its saving power. The Spirit of God transforms the life. We put away sinful thoughts and renounce evil deeds. Love, humility, and peace take the place of anger, envy, and strife. Joy takes the place of sadness. When by faith we surrender to God, the power that no human eye can see creates a new being in the image of God. We may know the beginning of redemption here, through personal experience. Its results reach through eternal ages. . . .

While Jesus was speaking, some gleams of truth penetrated the ruler's mind. Yet he did not fully understand the Savior's words. He said wonderingly, "How can these things be?"

"Are you the teacher of Israel, and do not know these things?" Jesus asked. Instead of feeling irritated over Jesus' plain words of truth, Nicodemus should have had a humble opinion of himself because of his spiritual ignorance. Yet Christ spoke with such solemn dignity and earnest love that Nicodemus was not offended. . . .

There was no excuse for Israel's blindness regarding the work of regeneration. David had prayed, "Create in me a clean heart, O God, and renew a steadfast spirit within me." Through Ezekiel God had promised, "I will give you a new heart and put a new spirit within you; I will take the heart of stone out of your flesh and give you a heart of flesh. I will put My Spirit within you and cause you to walk in My statutes.". . .

Nicodemus now began to comprehend the meaning of these scriptures. He saw that the most rigid outward obedience to just the letter of the law could entitle no one to enter the kingdom of heaven.

Nicodemus was being drawn to Christ. As the Savior explained the new birth to him, he longed for this change in himself. How could it take place? Jesus answered his unspoken question: "As Moses lifted up the serpent in the wilderness, even so must the Son of Man be lifted up, that whoever believes in Him should not perish but have eternal life."

The symbol of the uplifted serpent made the Savior's mission plain to Nicodemus. When the people of Israel were dying from the sting of the fiery serpents, God directed Moses to make a serpent of bronze and place it high in the middle of the congregation. All who would look at it would live. The serpent was a symbol of Christ. As the image made in the likeness of the destroying serpents was lifted up for their healing, so One made "in the likeness of sinful flesh" was to be their Redeemer. Romans 8:3. God wanted to lead the Israelites to the Savior. Whether to heal their wounds or pardon their sins, they could do nothing for themselves but show their faith in the Gift of God. They were to look and live.

Those who had been bitten by the serpents might have demanded a scientific explanation of how looking would heal them. But no explanation was given. To refuse to look was to die. Nicodemus received the lesson and carried it with him. He searched the Scriptures in a new way, not for discussion but to receive life for the soul. He submitted to the leading of the Holy Spirit.

Thousands today need to learn the same truth Nicodemus learned from the uplifted serpent. "There is no other name under heaven given among men by which we must be saved." Acts 4:12. Through faith we receive the grace of God, but faith is not our Savior. It earns nothing. It is the hand by which we lay hold on Christ, who is the remedy for sin. We cannot even repent without the aid of the Spirit of God. The Scripture says of Christ, "Him God has exalted to His right hand to be Prince and Savior, to give repentance to Israel and forgiveness of sins." Acts 5:31. Repentance comes from Christ as truly as does pardon.

How, then, are we to be saved? "Behold! The Lamb of God who takes away the sin of the world!" John 1:29. The light shining from the cross reveals the love of God. His love is drawing us to Himself. If we do not resist this drawing, we will be led to the foot of the cross in repentance for the sins that have crucified the Savior. Then through faith the Spirit of God produces a new life in the soul. He brings the thoughts and desires into obedience to Christ. He creates the heart and the mind anew in the image of Jesus, who works in us to subdue all things to Himself. Then He writes the law of God in the mind and heart, and we can say with Christ, "I delight to do Your will, O my God." Psalm 40:8.

In the conversation with Nicodemus, Jesus unfolded the plan of salvation. In none of His later instruction did He explain so fully, step by step, the work necessary to be done in the hearts of all who wish to inherit the kingdom of heaven. At the very beginning of His ministry, He opened the truth to a member of the Sanhedrin, an appointed teacher of the people. But the leaders of Israel did not welcome the light. Nicodemus hid the truth in his heart, and for three years there was little apparent fruit.

But the words Jesus spoke at night on the lonely mountain were not lost. In the Sanhedrin council, Nicodemus repeatedly defeated plans to destroy Jesus. When at last He was lifted up on the cross, Nicodemus remembered, "As Moses lifted up the serpent in the wilderness, even so must the Son of Man be lifted up, that whoever believes in Him should not perish but have eternal life." The light from that secret meeting illuminated the cross of Calvary, and Nicodemus saw in Jesus the world's Redeemer.

After the Lord ascended, when persecution scattered the disciples, Nicodemus came forward boldly. He used his wealth to sustain the infant church that the Jews had expected to disappear at the death of Christ. In the time of danger, he who had been so cautious and questioning was firm as a rock, encouraging the faith of the disciples and furnishing funds to carry forward the work of the gospel. He became poor in this world's goods, but he never hesitated in the faith that had its beginning in that nighttime conference with Jesus.

Nicodemus told John the story of that interview, and John recorded it for the instruction of millions. The truths taught there are as important today as they were on that solemn night on the shadowy mountain, when the Jewish ruler came to learn the way of life from the lowly Teacher of Galilee.[4]

1. Ellen G. White, *The Desire of Ages* (Mountain View, CA: Pacific Press®, 1940), 138.

2. White, 139, 140.

3. White, 167.

4. Ellen G. White, *Humble Hero* (Nampa, ID: Pacific Press®, 2009), 70–74; reprinted by permission from the Ellen G. White Estate.

5

The Testimony of the Samaritans

E. Edward Zinke

John's description of Jesus' visit to Samaria will be enlightened by briefly discussing the history of Samaria. After the death of King Solomon, the kingdom of Israel was divided over a lack of agreement on taxation. Solomon's son Rehoboam became king of the Southern Kingdom, the territories of the tribes of Judah and Benjamin.

Under Jeroboam, the Northern Kingdom took over the other ten tribes. It became idolatrous, wavering in its fidelity to God's Word. Later, Jezebel, Ahab's wife, brought idolatry to the country. She built a temple to Baal and brought its worship to the Northern Kingdom. The worship of Asherah was also encouraged. The prophets of God, including Elijah and Elisha, preached with great fervor against the pagan influences.

The Northern Kingdom's capital city, Samaria, was well built with fine fortifications. It stood for roughly 150 years until the Assyrians destroyed it. When the city fell, around thirty thousand citizens were carried away from the area. It was later repopulated by people from Babylonia and Syria.

Alexander the Great occupied the city of Samaria in 333 BC. He set up a governor who was later killed by the Samaritans. Alexander punished the population by removing them to Shechem, and then he replaced them with Macedonians. Notice again that the original population was largely displaced and the city reinhabited by populations foreign to the lineage of Abraham.[1]

During the time of Ezra and Nehemiah, many Jews were able to return to Jerusalem. When the rebuilding of the walls of the city commenced, the nearby inhabitants of Samaria, led by Sanballat, offered their help. When they were turned down, they did their best to destroy or delay the project. Sanballat used all kinds of threats, slander, and lies to stop the project. But God led and protected His people through the leadership of Ezra and Nehemiah.

The journey through Samaria

Jesus and His disciples went to Judea and were baptizing there. They were baptizing more individuals than John the Baptist and his disciples, who were also baptizing nearby. This created tension between the disciples of John and the disciples of Christ. Some Jews hoped to use this situation to create animosity between the two groups.[2] But John the Baptist was very forthright in answering their challenges:

> "A man can receive nothing unless it has been given to him from heaven. You yourselves bear me witness, that I said, 'I am not the Christ,' but, 'I have been sent before Him.' He who has the bride is the bridegroom; but the friend of the bridegroom, who stands and hears him, rejoices greatly because of the bridegroom's voice. Therefore this joy of mine is fulfilled. He must increase, but I must decrease. He who comes from above is above all;

he who is of the earth is earthly and speaks of the earth. He who comes from heaven is above all. . . . The Father loves the Son, and has given all things into His hand. He who believes in the Son has everlasting life; and he who does not believe the Son shall not see life, but the wrath of God abides on him" (John 3:27–31, 35, 36).

Soon after this furor, Jesus departed for Galilee to avoid conflict. The most direct route was through Samaria. As noted, Samaria was not a friendly place. The split between the Northern and Southern Kingdoms after the death of Solomon left the two peoples at odds with each other. The rift between the two nations grew even tenser with the building of the temple upon the return from the Babylonian captivity. As a result, the Jews avoided traveling through Samaria whenever possible. The inhabitants of Samaria were a mixed breed in culture and religion. The citizens were descendants of people who had lived in many different countries. Thus, the Samaritans were a mix of many different religions.

The woman at the well

On their way to Sychar, Jesus and His disciples passed by "the plot of ground that Jacob gave to his son Joseph. Now Jacob's well was there" (John 4:5, 6). Jesus was tired and sat down by Himself on the curbstone of the well while the disciples continued to the city.

While Jesus sat at the well around noon, in the heat of the day, a woman came out of the city to fill her water pot. Jesus wanted to reach this woman, and it is worth noting the method by which He did so. He did not begin with a discussion of Daniel 7 or even of Isaiah 53. Instead of preaching, He asked a favor. He requested a drink of water.

The woman was surprised. Even in a difficult situation, a Jew would not ask a favor of a Samaritan. But here was a Man asking this favor of—can you imagine!—a Samaritan woman. And not only that, a woman of ill repute, as will be seen.

Herein, Jesus gave an example of witnessing. Instead of preaching, He asked a favor. Who would turn down a request for a drink of water in this arid landscape?

This opened the door for further dialogue. Jesus told her, "If you knew the gift of God, and who it is who says to you, 'Give Me a drink,' you would have asked Him, and He would have given you living water" (John 4:10).

Now the woman asked the impossible question: How could this Man obtain water with no vessel to contain it?

Jesus answered, "Whoever drinks of this water will thirst again, but whoever drinks of the water that I shall give him will never thirst. But the water that I shall give him will become in him a fountain of water springing up into everlasting life" (verses 13, 14).

The woman immediately asked Christ to give her this living water so that she would not need to come and draw from the well anymore.

Jesus reveals His divinity

Jesus asked the woman to bring her husband.

She responded that she had no husband.

Then Jesus revealed her secret: she had already had five husbands and now lived with one who was not her husband.

At this, the woman stated that Jesus was a prophet. This gave her the opportunity to divert the narrative from an embarrassing conversation about herself and have a longtime question answered. She said her ancestors had worshiped on this mountain (Mount Gerizim), but the Jews had said that worship must be in Jerusalem.

Jesus answered, "Woman, believe Me, the hour is coming when you will neither on this mountain, nor in Jerusalem, worship the Father. You worship what you do not know; we know what we worship, for salvation is of the Jews. But the hour is coming, and now is, when the true worshipers will worship the Father in spirit and truth; for the Father is seeking such to worship Him. God is Spirit, and those who worship Him must worship in spirit and truth" (verses 21–24).

Worship is not limited to specific locations or ethnicities. True worship takes place in spirit and in truth.

The woman then declared that she knew that the Messiah was coming and would tell all things.

Jesus responded that it was He, the Messiah, who was speaking with her.

Then the woman left her water pot—that is, her entire past—and ran into the city, proclaiming that she had met a Man who told her all that she ever did. She asked whether this could be the Messiah.

Meanwhile, the disciples were returning from town. They offered food to Jesus.

He answered that His food was "to do the will" of Him who sent Him and "to finish His work" (verse 34). He went on to warn against waiting too long for the harvest—the salvation of people—for the fields were ready for harvest. Jesus was speaking about the reception that they were receiving in Samaria.

Many of the Samaritans believed because of the testimony of the woman. Jesus stayed two more days, and many more believed because of His ministry.

And now comes the climax of the story. The villagers remarked to the woman, "Now we believe, not because of what you said, for we ourselves have heard Him and we know that this is indeed the Christ, the Savior of the world" (verse 42).

The human heart

John must have been thrilled as he wrote this passage, for it contains the essence of why he wrote his account: "Truly Jesus did many other signs in the presence of His disciples, which are not written in this book; but these are written that you may believe that Jesus is the Christ, the Son of God, and that believing you may have life in His name" (John 20:30, 31). And John was writing his Gospel not just for Nathanael, Nicodemus, the Samaritan woman, or the nobleman and his family—he was writing it for you and for me. Today, we hear the invitation, and now is the time to accept Christ's call.

In the stories of the Samaritan woman (John 4:7–30), Nathanael (John 1:45–51), Nicodemus (John 3:1–21), and the nobleman whose son was healed (John 4:46–53), we find that Jesus knows the deepest thoughts of a human being. In John 2, during the Passover attended by Christ and His disciples, John notes this truth: "Now when He was in Jerusalem at the Passover, during the feast, many believed in His name when they saw the signs which He did. But Jesus did not commit Himself to them, because He knew all men, and had no need that anyone should testify of man, for He knew what was in man" (verses 23–25). Jesus did not commit Himself to the crowds at the temple because He knew what was in humankind.

This theme that Christ knows what is in the human heart runs through the Gospel of John. Nathanael doubted that any good thing could come out of Nazareth, yet Jesus saw him as an Israelite in whom there was no guile. Nicodemus did not recognize his need for rebirth, and Christ called him out for it. The woman at the well doubted that Christ could deliver on His promise to provide springs of living water, and the nobleman initially needed empirical evidence before he would believe in Christ.

John's message in each case is that Jesus knows what is in our hearts. He stands there, ready to lead us out from that which separates us from Him.

A mosaic of themes

While John specifically declared that he chose signs as a theme for his Gospel, there are a number of other themes that he used to make his point about who Jesus is. These themes are mutually developed and so crafted that they intertwine with each other in a beautiful pattern, in a mosaic that enriches the Gospel of John. The beautiful truth is that we can know Jesus is the Christ, and with that knowledge, we can have life through His name.

Themes in John 4

Water	Jesus requested a drink at Jacob's well (John 4:6–14). Water is necessary for life. It quenches thirst, and it cleanses. This theme is first seen in the rite of baptism, administered by John the Baptist in John 1:26–33.
Truth	Jesus is the Truth. He stated that worship must be in spirit and truth (John 4:23, 24). The theme of truth is first seen in John 1:1.
Holy Spirit	Again, Jesus stated that worship must be in spirit and truth (John 4:23, 24). The theme of the Holy Spirit is first seen in John 1:32, 33.

Themes in the Gospel of John

Testimony	Jesus testified of Himself as the Messiah (John 4:26, 41). The woman at the well testified to the Samaritans (verses 28, 29, 39, 42). The Samaritan villagers testified that Jesus was the Messiah (verse 42). This theme of testimony is first seen in John 1:6–8.
Bread, food	The disciples had gone into the Samarian city to buy food (John 4:8, 31–34). The theme of bread, or food, first appears in John 4:8.

---

1. *The Seventh-day Adventist Bible Dictionary*, rev. ed., Commentary Reference Series, vol. 8 (Washington, DC: Review and Herald®, 1979), s.v. "Samaria."

2. Ellen G. White, *The Desire of Ages* (Mountain View, CA: Pacific Press®, 1940), 178–180.

6

More Testimonies About Jesus

E. Edward Zinke

Beyond the signs of Christ's divinity, John recorded other themes that enrich the message of his book. In particular, he notes signs that have a distinct Messianic character. They point to Jesus as the Christ—the fulfillment of the Old Testament promises of a coming Savior who would bring salvation to those who accepted it.

John wants his readers to understand that Jesus is the Messiah. He wants us to accept Him as our Savior so that we can have salvation through Him.

The early signs of Christ's divinity that John recorded in his Gospel include Jesus changing water to wine, healing the nobleman's child, healing the man by the pool of Bethesda, feeding the five thousand, healing the man blind from birth, and resurrecting Lazarus. Although other miracles are mentioned, we have reviewed these because they are specifically labeled by John as signs.

Additionally, we have studied the witnesses who testified about Jesus in the Gospel of John. They are a diverse group and include John the Baptist, the Holy Spirit, Andrew, Philip, Nicodemus, the woman at the well, the people of Samaria, and Jesus' own testimony about Himself.

In each case, there were those who submitted to the Word of God and therefore accepted Jesus Christ as their Savior. Others held to their worldview as the measure of all things and rejected Jesus as a result.

Early in Christ's ministry, there was a general acceptance of the meaning of the signs. Many affirmed that He was the Messiah. But soon a reaction began and with it a divergence of opinion. The healing of the man by the pool of Bethesda caused many leaders to reject the message that Jesus is the Messiah, sent from God the Father. They rebuffed Him as their Savior because He did not fit their mold, their expectations, of what the Messiah would be. He was not a conquering hero who would overcome their problems with Rome. Even the testimony of Moses, their hero, was not enough to convince the ruling class otherwise.

John the Baptist testifies again

Though Jesus was largely rejected, John is careful to include the testimonies of many who believed in the Messiah. Besides Andrew, Philip, and the woman at the well, other witnesses stepped up to declare that Jesus was the Christ. John the Baptist, a key witness in the Gospel of John, was given a prophetic role to pave the way for the coming and reception of the Messiah (John 1:6–8, 15, 19–36).

John seldom brings a person on stage more than once, but John the Baptist is an exception. He appears in John's Gospel in chapters 1, 3, and 5. His testimony is a very strong witness of Jesus as the Messiah.

Standing by the river Jordan, John the Baptist saw Jesus coming toward him and said,

> "Behold! The Lamb of God who takes away the sin of the world! This is He of whom I said, 'After me comes a Man who is preferred before me, for He was before me.' I did not know Him; but that He should be revealed to Israel, therefore I came baptizing with water."
>
> And John bore witness, saying, "I saw the Spirit descending from heaven like a dove, and He remained upon Him. I did not know Him, but He who sent me to baptize with water said to me, 'Upon whom you see the Spirit descending, and remaining on Him, this is He who baptizes with the Holy Spirit.' And I have seen and testified that this is the Son of God" (John 1:29–34).

In John 3, John was baptizing near where the disciples of Jesus were also baptizing. A quarrel came up between the two camps over who was baptizing more disciples. Apparently, the Jewish leaders saw this as an opportunity to foment division between the two groups. This tension allowed John the Baptist to de-escalate the feud and describe the differences between Jesus and himself. His primary job was to prepare the way for the Messiah to come, describe who Jesus was, and build Him up.

John the Baptist humbly dealt with the quarrel between the two parties while magnifying Christ at the same time. He made it clear that he was not the Christ. Rather, he was the forerunner of Christ. Like the relationship between a bridegroom and his friend, John the Baptist stated, "He must increase, but I must decrease" (verse 30).

A greater witness

In John 5, the witness of John the Baptist is mentioned for the third time. He was a witness to the truth. As a burning and shining lamp, his testimony was heard for a short time. Jesus carefully reminded the leaders that their initial interest in John's message had subsided. He then introduced them to a witness greater than John the Baptist—the witness of His Father.

He declared that the works that the Father sent Him to perform bore witness that the Father had sent Him. "I have a greater witness than John's; for the works which the Father has given Me to finish—the very works that I do—bear witness of Me, that the Father has sent Me" (verse 36). Another testimony was that of the Father Himself: He "who sent Me, has testified of Me. You have neither heard His voice at any time, nor seen His form" (verse 37).

Now comes an important rebuke: the rulers have rejected the testimony of Scripture—the means by which God has chosen to communicate with us and draw us close to Himself. The Scriptures testify of Jesus in order that, by accepting His invitation, we may have eternal life. If we reject Scripture's invitation to enter a love relationship with God, how can we know the God who offers Himself to us through His Word?

The witness of the multitude

The Gospel of John then moves to the miracle of the feeding of the five thousand (John 6). This miracle, or sign, took place when Jesus was preaching in the countryside. There was no access to food except for five loaves and two fish from a boy's lunch. With these meager resources, Jesus fed five thousand people.

This miracle was seen as a sign that Jesus was called to a prophetic ministry. In fact, this miracle was seen as the fulfillment of the promise of the coming of "the Prophet" (John 1:21; 6:14). Surely this was the fulfillment of the prophecies that a Deliverer would come and free the people. Unfortunately, this attitude toward the Messianic mission came from a worldly perspective. It shaped the people's thoughts about who the Redeemer was and what He would do.

The Jewish people had assumed that Moses had delivered the manna in the wilderness and that Jesus could also provide bread. The crowd, anxious to move forward with this idea, asked for a sign like that which Moses had given in the wilderness. They were not wasting any time in vetting Jesus to determine whether He was up to the job.

The crowds flocked to see Jesus the next day. But remember, Jesus knows what is in the human heart. He stated, "Most assuredly, I say to you, you seek Me, not because you saw the signs, but because you ate of the loaves and were filled. Do not labor for the food which perishes, but for the food which endures to everlasting life, which the Son of Man will give you, because God the Father has set His seal on Him" (verses 26, 27).

He declared Himself to be the Bread of Life through whom was eternal life. The manna in the wilderness merely sustained temporal life. Jesus said, "Moses did not give you the bread from heaven, but My Father gives you the true bread from heaven" (verse 32). In other words, He, Jesus, was the Bread from heaven. He was the miracle they were seeking, but they did not recognize it.

Christ went on to state, "The bread of God is He who comes down from heaven and gives life to the world" (verse 33).

The crowd answered, "Give us this bread" (verse 34).

Jesus said, "I am the bread of life. He who comes to Me shall never hunger, and he who believes in Me shall never thirst" (verse 35).

"The Jews then complained about Him, because He said, 'I am the bread which came down from heaven' " (verse 41). They rejected Him when they realized that He would not become their earthly king. He did not fit the mold produced by earthly thinking and circumstances. They refused the conversion that would transform their thinking so that they could recognize and accept Jesus as the Messiah.

In John's account, there is often a response of faith and a contrasting response of doubt. Regardless of the response, Jesus' desire is the same for everyone: "This is the will of Him who sent Me, that everyone who sees the Son and believes in Him may have everlasting life; and I will raise him up at the last day" (verse 40).

The testimony of Peter

John the Baptist declared Jesus to be the Lamb of God. This statement clearly referred to the sacrificial system that provided atonement for one's personal sins in order to be reconciled to God.

By saying that He would give them His flesh to eat, Jesus hoped that they would understand His role as the Lamb of God. "I am the living bread which came down from heaven. If anyone eats of this bread, he will live forever; and the bread that I shall give is My flesh, which I shall give for the life of the world" (verse 51).

But they failed to make the connection and grumbled instead, saying, "How can this Man give us His flesh to eat?" (verse 52).

> The reference to eating Jesus's flesh and drinking His blood must have shocked the Jews. They knew He could not be taken literally . . . , yet that seems to be the natural sense of His words. The eating and drinking spoken of here are to be understood as a strong and vivid metaphor to denote the believer's complete appropriation of Jesus

> by faith. . . . There is also a connection in His words with the Lord's Supper. When we participate in the emblems of the ritual, we are symbolically eating the flesh and drinking the blood of Jesus—appropriating the benefits of His death for us—in order to renew our complete commitment to Him. His sacrificial death continues to nurture our spiritual life.[1]

Because the multitude misunderstood that Jesus was the true Lamb of God, they rejected Him. He was also rejected by the listeners whom He taught in the synagogue at Capernaum. In addition, He was aware that some of His disciples were murmuring and that one would betray Him (verses 60–66, 70, 71).

Jesus then asked His immediate disciples whether they wanted to leave Him. He got an unbelievable response from Peter! This response was so strong that the apostle John must have been delighted to record it in his Gospel: "Lord, to whom shall we go? You have the words of eternal life. Also we have come to believe and know that You are the Christ, the Son of the living God" (verses 68, 69).

An appeal

John wants his readers to understand that Jesus is the Messiah. He wants us to accept Him as our personal Savior so that we might have salvation through Him. His Gospel describes the battle between biblical thinking and humanistic thinking. Is Jesus the promised Messiah, or is He just the most prominent person of the age? Is He clay in our hands, to be molded by the worldview of contemporary society? Is He to be understood from whatever worldview one may choose? Is He an idol for the age—a mere god who fits society's demands? Or is He the

Messiah whose coming was prophesied in the Old Testament?

The Gospel of John does not consider Jesus to be *a* messiah; rather, it considers Him to be *the* Messiah! The temptation in all ages has been to try to fit God into contemporary thinking—the hero, the savior of the age. But John is quite clear that there is only one Messiah, the Logos, the Son of God, God Himself from eternity to eternity, and therefore, the Savior of the world. The Only Begotten of the Father is Jesus Christ. He is not subject to any other system of thought. He is the foundation for all aspects of life, including our own limited thinking.

As we study these accounts, let us feel the heart of John, who is yearning to bring us to His Messiah. Let us sense the struggle between Christ and Satan, recognizing that Jesus invites us to be open to His ministry on our behalf. Let us be receptive to Him who desires to give us His victory right now and His presence throughout eternity!

---

1. Ángel Manuel Rodríguez, ed., *Andrews Bible Commentary*, vol. 2, *New Testament* (Berrien Springs, MI: Andrews University Press, 2022), 1431.

7

Blessed Are Those Who Believe

E. Edward Zinke

What does it mean when we say that salvation is by faith and not by works? Can we redefine faith so that it can morph into a work? If so, is salvation by works? The devil knows this is a serious topic, and he does not care how much faith we have, so long as we use his definition.

In John's Gospel, John recounted the signs that Jesus performed because they pointed to Jesus as the Messiah, the Savior of the world. But it is not enough to simply know something about Jesus. We must have faith that He is our personal Messiah, that He is the Son of God, and that we might have life through His name.

What is *faith*?

It is tempting to define faith from a humanistic perspective—that faith is built on rational-empirical evidence. And this evidence is the result of a scientific inquiry based on humanistic endeavors, without regard to the Holy Scriptures. The humanistic concept of faith can be outlined as follows:

> The process generally starts with doubt—attempting to prove the validity of an assertion in order to offer it as truth—as worthy of one's faith.
>
> It relies upon genius, creativity, initiative, freedom of exploration, and capabilities of mankind.
>
> It relies upon the five senses as a basis for collecting the relevant data.
>
> It looks for patterns and integrates the data and interprets it on the basis of a paradigm which interprets our common experience and understanding of the world.
>
> A hypothesis is formed which leads to testable predictions which results in a new round of observations.
>
> The result is a probability statement as to what things are like or as to how new pieces of data entering the system will relate to the old.
>
> In summary, the data is brought together in such a way as to yield a conclusion, a faith statement as to how things probably are. The conclusion is in the hand of mankind. It is under human control, it is a human achievement, and it is created upon a human basis such as reason or some other faculty of mankind.[1]

The biblical concept of faith is just the reverse. Faith is not a human creation; "it is the gift of God" (Ephesians 2:8). Faith does not rest on the wisdom of humankind but in "the power of God" (1 Corinthians 2:4, 5). Christ Himself is "the author and finisher of our faith" (Hebrews 12:2). The Spirit and Word work together. "No man can create faith. The Spirit operating upon and enlightening the human mind, creates faith in God. In the Scriptures faith is stated to be the gift of God, powerful unto salvation, enlightening the hearts of those who search for truth as for hidden treasure."[2]

Faith is not built upon an external foundation but is itself the assurance, the conviction, "the evidence of things not seen" (Hebrews 11:1). Faith in the Word of God is not based on humanly derived knowledge; rather, faith itself is the foundation of knowledge. "By faith we understand that the worlds were framed by the word of God" (verse 3). "Only in the light of revelation can it [nature] be read aright."[3] Faith is the basis for discerning between truth and error. "Faith comes by hearing, and hearing by the word of God" (Romans 10:17). The assurance and evidence for faith is God's Word. We walk by faith, not by sight (1 Corinthians 5:7). Attempting to use the data of reason as criteria for determining whether Scripture is the Word of God is to doubt that which has already been declared by God. It is similar to Christ's temptation in the wilderness—namely, to doubt that He was the Son of God after He had already been affirmed by the Word of God. "Genuine faith has its foundation in the promises and provisions of the Scriptures."[4]

Concerning faith, John calls upon many witnesses to make his point. Some of the witnesses responded in faith, and some responded with doubt.

Doubt in Eden

In the Bible, Eve is the first example of someone who was tempted to waver from allegiance to God's word. On what basis would she make her decision on how to relate to the tree in the center of the Garden? Satan started her out with doubt: "Has God not said . . . ?"

She then questioned the validity of God's word.

Next, she tried science. She gathered the evidence. The fruit looked good to eat. Furthermore, the serpent had partaken of it and appeared to have increased powers. *If I partake, I can also expect increased powers*, she thought.

She also appealed to philosophy: a god of love would not destroy a person whom he created nor would he withhold such beautiful fruit from his creatures.

In hindsight, her failed logic is easy to see, but how could she have come to the right conclusion and avoided disaster? By simply relying on the word of God.

The witness of Noah

In contrast to Eve, Noah is a shining example of someone who chose faith over sight.

> The wise men of this world talked of science and the fixed laws of nature, and declared that there could be no variation in these laws, and that this message of Noah could not possibly be true. The talented men of Noah's time set themselves in league against God's will and purpose, and scorned the message and the messenger that he had sent. When they could not move Noah from his firm and implicit trust in the word of God, they pointed to him as a fanatic, as a ranting old man, full of superstition and madness. Thus they condemned him because he would not be turned from his purpose by reasonings and theories of men. It was true that Noah could not controvert their philosophies, or refute the claims of science so called; but he could proclaim the word of God; for he knew it contained the infinite wisdom of the Creator, and, as he sounded it everywhere, it lost none of its force and reality because men of the world treated him with ridicule and contempt.[5]

Noah's commitment to faith in the face of great odds continues to inspire us today. The word of God is more sure than human logic and scientific declarations. "We do not look at the things which are seen, but at the things which are not seen. For the things which are seen are temporary, but the things which are not seen are eternal" (2 Corinthians 4:18).

The witness of Abraham

Abraham is another patriarch who lived by faith. He exemplifies the best of those who have relationships with God. Although he fell from time to time, he repented of his failings and maintained his close relationship with God. As a result, God promised that Abraham's descendants would be like the sands of the sea and that the Savior would come through him.

> "By faith Abraham, when he was called to go out into a place which he should after receive for an inheritance, obeyed; and he went out, not knowing whither he went." Hebrews 11:8. Abraham's unquestioning obedience is one of the most striking evidences of faith to be found in all the Bible. To him, faith was "the substance of things hoped for, the evidence of things not seen." Verse 1. Relying upon the divine promise, without the least outward assurance of its fulfillment, he abandoned home and kindred and native land, and went forth, he knew not whither, to follow where God should lead.[6]

Abraham could not explain his course of action to his friends. Spiritual things are spiritually discerned, and his motives and actions were not comprehended by his idolatrous kindred.

Imagine Abraham standing before the church board in Ur of the Chaldeans. "I am planning on moving away."

"Oh, we will miss you. Where are you going?"

"I don't know!"

"And why are you doing something like this? We thought you were an intelligent man. We need you as our head elder here at the church in Ur!"

"But God has asked me to depart to a place that I do not know."

"It doesn't make any sense that God would ask someone to leave one of the most modern, sophisticated places in the world. You must have lost your mind. If God wants you to do evangelism, you have an audience right here. Have you checked to see who you would preach to?"

"I don't know!"

"A smart man would check that out first. It is only reasonable to know something more about the situation than 'I don't know!' Do you plan to have children? What would moving mean for them, their education, and their inheritance? Will you have any enemies there? You mean you have not checked that out either? How foolish!"

Notice how Abraham was operating under a different set of principles than his idolatrous relatives. From their perspective, he was stupid, backward, crazy, and deranged! He was using logic that did not make any sense. From Abraham's perspective, faith was the guide to live by.

Doubt at Kadesh Barnea

Unfortunately, Abraham's descendants—the children of Israel—did not possess his faith. When they were camped at Kadesh Barnea, Moses sent spies into Canaan in preparation for their entrance into the Promised Land (Numbers 13). The majority of the spies brought back a bad report. "The ten spies returned from Canaan doubting the command of God. No God in his right mind would take Israel into battle in Canaan. Fortified passes needed to be crossed, there were giants in the land, the armies were well equipped and trained, and there were great walls around the cities."[7]

The Israelites' reluctance to enter Canaan was catastrophic. Their doubt at this critical juncture meant that they missed out on the kingdom waiting for them. This doubt, which caused them to wander in the wilderness for forty more years, was similar to the doubt that existed in the time of Christ.

The opportunities of Pilate

The last chance for the children of Israel to realize their mission and salvage their destiny came during the final week of Christ's life. Pilate was a central character in the drama, and on many occasions during the trial, he had opportunities to accept Christ as the divine Son of God. Although he did not take advantage of these opportunities, his witness to who Jesus was provides important insights.

In a sense, Pilate was an impartial observer who was ensnared in a moment of Jewish political intrigue. He was caught in the middle. On the one hand, he represented Rome. Of course, the Jews were constantly attempting to undermine Roman rule. He had to be careful lest he become trapped on the wrong side. If he handled Jesus in a way that appeared he was supporting a Jewish attempt at rebellion, he would be in trouble.

On the other hand, Pilate's job was to keep the peace and maintain justice in the Jewish state. He could not execute someone just because it suited the prejudices of the Jewish rulers.

After Jesus was tried by Annas and Caiaphas, He was taken to Pilate, the Roman governor. At first, Pilate wished to charge the defendant and dispatch the case right away. But he became intrigued with the prisoner and asked penetrating questions.

Pilate asked a question regarding the offense of the prisoner.

The Jews answered by dodging the question. "If He were

not an evildoer, we would not have delivered Him up to you" (John 18:30).

Pilate recognized that this was a Jewish issue and immediately sent the case back to the Jewish leaders to adjudge.

The Jews answered that they could not lawfully put someone to death.

Pilate next asked Jesus if He was the King of the Jews.

Jesus clarified that His kingdom was not of this world.

Pilate then asked if He was a king.

Jesus responded that His kingdom was not of this world but that He should bear witness to the truth.

Pilate then asked, "What is truth?" (verse 38).

Unfortunately, the Truth was standing right there before him, and Pilate did not wait for a response.

Pilate then went out and reported that he found no fault in Him and asked the people whether he should release Jesus to them.

The crowd asked for Barabbas instead—a robber and a terrorist.

In desperation, Pilate brought Jesus out again, declaring that he found no fault in Him.

Jesus was presented again with a statement from Pilate: "Behold your King!" (John 19:14).

The chief priests declared that they had no king but Caesar.

And the Roman soldiers took Jesus and crucified Him.

Pilate put a title on the cross in three languages: "JESUS OF NAZARETH, THE KING OF THE JEWS" (verse 19).

The Jewish leaders attempted to change the wording, but Pilate declared that what he had written was written.

Notice how this narrative fits the purpose of the Gospel of John. Pilate, a Roman governor and judge, declares *three times* in favor of the Defendant: "I find no crime in him" (John

18:38; 19:4, 6, ASV). And these declarations were made in less-than-ideal circumstances for Pilate. These statements are important to the theme of John's Gospel because here is a Roman judge testifying to the righteousness of Jesus, who was the perfect Lamb of God. If one sin was in Jesus, He could not have secured the plan of salvation. It is significant to have Pilate's testimony with such emphasis!

Furthermore, the discussion with Pilate clarified the kingship of Jesus. He was not an earthly king. But He was a heavenly King and came to this earth to fulfill that role in the plan of salvation. Although Pilate never became a follower of Christ, he did play an important role in John's Gospel by declaring to have found no fault in Jesus.

The faithfulness of Christ

In stark contrast to Pilate, Christ had a deep faith in His Father. Though He was tempted to doubt His Father's will, He routinely relied on the Word of God.

In the wilderness of temptation, He could have used the tools of science to prove His divinity by turning stones into bread. He could have appealed to philosophy to doubt God's Word: Would God leave His Son in the wilderness for forty days without food and companionship? Instead, He answered with faith in the revealed Word of God: "It is written . . ." (Matthew 4:4, 7, 10).

Doubting Thomas

Finally, we come to the doubting disciple. On the evening of the same day as the Resurrection, Jesus came to the upper room where the disciples were gathered. Christ showed them the nail prints in His hands and the injury on His side, but Thomas happened to be absent.

When Thomas became aware of this encounter, he vowed not to believe that Christ was resurrected without seeing the prints in Jesus' hands and the injury on His side. The next week, Christ joined the disciples again. Thomas was there, and he responded: "My Lord and my God!" (John 20:28).

Jesus said to Thomas, "Because you have seen Me, you have believed. Blessed are those who have not seen and yet have believed" (verse 29). These words were addressed to Thomas, but they are meant for us. Although we have not witnessed the first-century Jesus, we can still accept Him as the promised Messiah. This is faith. This is ignoring the naysayers and trusting our lives to the Word of God in the here and now and in the hereafter.

---

1. E. Edward Zinke, "Faith-Science Issues: An Epistemological Perspective," *Journal of the Adventist Theological Society* 15, no. 1 (Spring 2004): 73.

2. Francis D. Nichol, ed., "Ellen G. White Comments," in *The Seventh-day Adventist Bible Commentary*, vol. 7 (Washington, DC: Review and Herald®, 1980), 940.

3. Ellen G. White, *The Faith I Live By* (Washington, DC: Review and Herald®, 1958), 24.

4. Ellen G. White, *The Desire of Ages* (Mountain View, CA: Pacific Press®, 1940), 126.

5. Ellen G. White, "An Example of Saving Faith," *Signs of the Times*, April 18, 1895.

6. Ellen G. White, *Patriarchs and Prophets* (Mountain View, CA: Pacific Press®, 1958), 126.

7. Zinke, "Faith-Science Issues," 71.

8

Fulfilling Old Testament Prophecies

Bill Knott

The last fifty years in the history of Western Christianity have been a time of tumultuous change and realignment. After nearly two millennia in which the Christian church anchored its assertions about the life, ministry, death, resurrection, and continuing ministry of Jesus in the authority of the received text of the Old and New Testaments, new methods of understanding Jesus have emerged—some of them with powerful societal impact.

At one end of the theological spectrum is the historical-critical method of studying the Bible, emerging from the Age of Enlightenment but honed in the mid-nineteenth century by European and American scholars. The historical-critical method deconstructed the received biblical text into an amalgam of different and sometimes even incompatible documents; each authored by a different and very human hand. This "higher criticism," as it came to be known, began with an essential doubt about the authenticity of the received text of both Old and New Testaments. It prioritized the human ability to assess, critique, and dismiss those portions of the Bible that it deemed of dubious origin or, to those employing it, seemed inconsistent with their vision of the authors' original intent. One well-known illustration of this "demythologizing" trend is the work of the Jesus Seminar, which gained international attention from the annual meeting of its members. They would vote by colored bead on the presumed authenticity of the sayings of Jesus recorded in the Gospels. In one famous decision, the Jesus Seminar concluded that only the phrase "Our Father" in what Christians have known as the Lord's Prayer could reliably be identified with an actual saying of Jesus.

The Jesus movement

Another trend emerging half a century ago was nearly an equal-and-opposite reaction to what it deemed a preoccupation of Christian scholars with the text of Scripture. The Jesus movement, which emerged from revival movements begun in the social tumult of the 1960s, brought hundreds of thousands of former social rebels and freethinkers into the orbit of Christian faith in the early 1970s. Churches, educational institutions, and even seminaries soon were filled with hundreds of passionate, committed young-adult Christians who placed great emphasis on the story of their personal experience of Jesus. For these seekers, their dynamic relationship with the risen Jesus superseded the biblical record of His life, ministry, death, and resurrection. The Jesus to whom they attached brought coherence to their 1970s lives, which had seemed incoherent in the 1960s. To them, Jesus was chiefly a figure to be worshiped, praised, and followed.

Streams emerging from the Jesus movement flowed into the faith communities of Christianity with revitalizing power; hundreds of persons prepared for pastoral ministry, planted new congregations, and brought new focus to Christ's call to discipleship. Many of these individuals gave deep and focused attention to the biblical revelation of Jesus. Others continued to emphasize primarily the relational aspects of Jesus, including personal devotion, practicing simple lives, and underlining the role of the Spirit in creating fresh, new communities that were relevant to the places in which they were planted.

Throughout this season, Pentecostalism steadily advanced. Its primary focus was on the subjective experience of Jesus as Savior and included a highly emotional worship style; the witness of miracles; and the phenomenon of glossolalia, or speaking in tongues.

Devaluing the Bible

It should surprise no one that elements of each of these phenomena also emerged in the worldwide movement of Seventh-day Adventists. Some Adventist scholars, trained in historical-critical methods of Bible study, have challenged the historicity and even the authenticity of the biblical documents upon which the Seventh-day Adventist Church made its first faith statements in the mid-nineteenth century. The impact on thousands of Adventist college students has moved many away from faith in the Bible—and even in the God who declares Himself to be revealed in its pages.

Conversely, a surging neo-Pentecostal focus on knowing Jesus experientially has caused tens of thousands of others to devalue the biblical revelation that assures us of His historical reality, His divine character, the truthfulness of His teachings, the attestations of His miracles, and the proofs of His resurrection. Discouraged by what they view as too great a focus on reading the Bible for information instead of knowing Jesus as a personal Savior, movements have arisen within Adventism in the last twenty years that promise to focus on Jesus only.

A full reading of John's Gospel is thus uniquely helpful in connecting Jesus to the enduring witness of the Old Testament regarding His coming life and ministry and offering an unparalleled witness to the powerful experience of knowing Jesus personally. The well-known narratives of Jesus' encounters with Nicodemus (chapter 3), the Samaritan woman at the well (chapter 4), the disabled man beside the pool of Bethesda (chapter 5), the man born blind (chapter 9), and with Mary and Martha who are mourning for Lazarus (chapter 11) anchor John's witness in a face-to-face, one-on-one experience of knowing Jesus as the divine Son of God, as the One who can forgive great sin, as a healer sent from God, and as the Lord who alone can raise the dead.

The reliability of the Old Testament

John's Gospel, almost certainly written after the synoptic Gospels of Matthew, Mark, and Luke, is his unique and personal witness to his experience of walking and talking with Jesus: "This is the disciple who is testifying to these things and has written them, and we know that his testimony is true" (John 21:24, NRSV). John unapologetically alerts his readers that his Gospel is a selection from among many other true narratives that could have been recorded: "And there are also many other things that Jesus did, which if they were written one by one, I suppose that even the world itself could not contain the books that would be written" (verse 25). John thus assumes that his readers will already be well acquainted with the narratives of Matthew, Mark, and Luke and will trust them as authentic.

But it is John's persistent and untiring effort to show us Jesus as the fulfillment, even the embodiment, of dozens of

Old Testament prophecies and statements that should forever silence those who attempt an unbiblical separation of the witness of both testaments. John might well agree with the concept that has found expression in the phrase "Jesus only"—so long as we include in the "only" the totality of the Old Testament witness to the person and ministry of Jesus and John's robust pictures of Him. The "only" of John's witness to Jesus is dramatically inclusive, not exclusive: John will not rest until readers have noted how rich is the witness of the Old Testament to the story of Jesus.

John anchors the witness of Jesus firmly in trusting the veracity and reliability of the Old Testament. In a famous rebuke to the scribes and Pharisees who consistently attempt to read Him out of the text, Jesus asserts, "You search the Scriptures, for in them you think you have eternal life; and these are they which testify of Me. But you are not willing to come to Me that you may have life" (John 5:39, 40). Jesus thus strongly implies that it is their unwillingness to see what is obvious in the text that prevents them from acknowledging His role as Messiah. According to Jesus, their refusal to accept His divine origin requires them to devalue the writings of Moses, which they claim as the supreme authority for their faith: "Do not think that I will accuse you before the Father; your accuser is Moses, on whom you have set your hope. If you believed Moses, you would believe me, for he wrote about me. But if you do not believe what he wrote, how will you believe what I say?" (verses 45–47, NRSV). The refusal to see what Scripture has made plain points to deeply held prejudice and hypocrisy, not a lack of convicting information.

In this decisive passage, Jesus echoes the lesson He will attempt to teach to the two disciples on the Emmaus Road on the day of His resurrection. Luke, whose narrative of Jesus was undoubtedly known to John, records that Jesus responded to their inability to connect the dots of the biblical witness by writing: "Then He said to them, 'O foolish ones, and slow of heart to believe in all that the prophets have spoken! Ought not the Christ to have suffered these things and to enter into His glory?' And beginning at Moses and all the Prophets, He expounded to them in all the Scriptures the things concerning Himself" (Luke 24:25–27). Unwillingness to see Jesus fully depicted in the text of the Old Testament is thus, according to Jesus, the result of deliberate refusal, foolishness, or lack of diligent study.

No book could fully illumine the many, many citations and allusions to the Old Testament on which John anchors his witness to Jesus. As previously noted, John himself reaches for exaggerated language to underscore the impossibility of the task: "I suppose that even the world itself could not contain the books that would be written" (John 21:25).

Yet even a brief overview of more than 100 such citations and allusions reminds us that John fully expects his readers to be fully conversant with the witness of the Old Testament. Much as with his other great work—the biblical book of Revelation—it is impossible to both read and understand his work unless you are willing to see the deep connections between the Old Testament and the ministry of Jesus—on Earth and in heaven. Some authors refer to this method as *intertextuality*—the deliberate construction or arrangement of a text to cite, echo, allude to, or parallel another existing work. In virtually everything he writes about Jesus in his Gospel, John assumes that his readers will "hear" the echo of what was the only known testament in his era.

An average of five allusions or citations of the Old Testament occur in each of the twenty-one chapter divisions of John's

Gospel. These include the conscious parallel construction of John's opening lines with those of the first lines of the book of Genesis. John is deliberately placing his account of Jesus in the context of the most momentous things that have ever occurred in the history of the world. "In the beginning God created the heavens and the earth" (Genesis 1:1) can be heard echoing through John's equally momentous announcement: "In the beginning was the Word, and the Word was with God, and the Word was God. He was in the beginning with God. All things were made through Him, and without Him nothing was made that was made" (John 1:1–3).

From John in his first epistle, we hear the attestation that the Jesus with whom he walked and talked was the cosmic Lord of all: "That which was from the beginning, which we have heard, which we have seen with our eyes, which we have looked upon, and our hands have handled, concerning the Word of life—the life was manifested, and we have seen, and bear witness, and declare to you" (1 John 1:1, 2). John likewise affirms the central truth that God—whose glory did not allow Him to be looked upon (Exodus 33:20: "He said, 'You cannot see My face; for no man shall see Me, and live' ")—is only knowable in the person of Jesus: "No one has seen God at any time. The only begotten Son, who is in the bosom of the Father, He has declared Him" (John 1:18).

These are not casual or incidental allusions; these are theological affirmations of the first order and are essential, John tells us, to correctly understand the totality of God and His revelation in Jesus.

John also links the ministry of John the Baptist to the work of the promised Messiah of the Old Testament. When questioned about his identity, the Baptist replied,

"I am

> 'The voice of one crying in the wilderness:
> "Make straight the way of the LORD," '

as the prophet Isaiah said" (verse 23).

The quotation of Isaiah 40, while not exact, is intended by John to unmistakably link the totality of the Messiah's ministry, which is prefigured in the book of Isaiah.

John the Baptist also made explicit the identification of Jesus as the Sin Bearer prefigured in Isaiah 53. Isaiah wrote:

> All we like sheep have gone astray;
> We have turned, every one, to his own way;
> And the LORD has laid on Him the iniquity of us all.
> He was oppressed and He was afflicted,
> Yet He opened not His mouth;
> He was led as a lamb to the slaughter (Isaiah 53:6, 7).

The Gospel writer John quotes John the Baptist as saying, "Behold! The Lamb of God who takes away the sin of the world!" (John 1:29). "And looking at Jesus as He walked, he said, 'Behold the Lamb of God!' " (verse 36).

I will draw all men to Me

To Nicodemus—perhaps the most biblically literate individual with whom Jesus ever conversed—Jesus associates Himself with the serpent lifted up on a pole for the healing of dying Israelites. Moses himself records that he "made a bronze serpent, and put it on a pole; and so it was, if a serpent had bitten anyone, when he looked at the bronze serpent, he lived"

(Numbers 21:9). Clearly prefiguring the manner in which He would die on a cross to save those snakebit by sin, Jesus tells this learned Torah scholar, "And as Moses lifted up the serpent in the wilderness, even so must the Son of Man be lifted up" (John 3:14). "And I, if I am lifted up from the earth, will draw all peoples to Myself" (John 12:32).

With the apostle Paul, whose witness to Jesus was also anchored in the Old Testament, John would affirm: "He is the image of the invisible God, the firstborn over all creation. For by Him all things were created that are in heaven and that are on earth, visible and invisible, whether thrones or dominions or principalities or powers. All things were created through Him and for Him. And He is before all things, and in Him all things consist" (Colossians 1:15–17).

9

The Source of Life

E. Edward Zinke and Kiersten Zinke

Some people say that life on this planet developed over millions of years, and the first forms of life started from chemicals in lakes and tidal pools. They think that we evolved from there to self-replicating nucleic acids to a primitive cell and finally to human beings. This belief is called the theory of evolution. Evolution takes God completely out of the process of creation.

Some say that God guided the process of evolution; this is called theistic evolution. And others say that we were created by the hand of God during Creation week a short time ago, just as the Bible says.

What difference does it make in what we think of our origins? Why can we not simply choose one of these models or make up another?

Our concept of creation affects how we see everything in the universe—our concept of God, ourselves, our fellow humans, the natural world, and how we are to live now and in the future. The doctrine of creation affects our entire worldview—from our past to the future. Creation, in fact, is a doctrine, but these days, it seems that almost no one considers doctrine important. But Jesus did! In John 17:3, He said that salvation is knowing Him: "This is eternal life, that they may know You, the only true God, and Jesus Christ whom You have sent."

The book of Hosea says something similar. Hosea was asked to marry Gomer, who was a woman of ill repute. Hosea's relationship with Gomer was a reflection of the Israelites' relationship with God. They would lust after pagan gods and then come back to God, only to wander away again and again. God was constantly wooing them to Himself.

> "I will betroth you to Me forever;
> Yes, I will betroth you to Me
> In righteousness and justice,
> In lovingkindness and mercy;
> I will betroth you to Me in faithfulness,
> And you shall *know* the LORD" (Hosea 2:19, 20; emphasis added).

God was constantly calling the Israelites to come to Him. He was inviting the Israelites to a relationship filled with knowledge about who He is.

Christianity is a relationship with God and Jesus Christ. But it is more than a relationship. Hosea 2:20 says, "And you shall *know* the LORD." Knowing has something to do with doctrine. Doctrine is teaching. It tells us about God so that we can truly *know* Him and *know* who He is!

In addition to knowledge of the other person, there are other key aspects to close relationships. It is important not only to know the other person but also to understand ourselves and the proper relationship between us. Doctrine tells us about ourselves and how to relate to God. It tells us who God is, who we are, and how we as humans are to relate to God and the rest of humankind.

Knowing God is also important because our lives are shaped by the people or things we admire the most. If we admire God the most, we will be transformed into His image, which will enable us to have an even closer relationship with Him. Doctrine is not an end in itself. It has meaning only if it leads to a mature relationship with our Creator God, who has revealed Himself in the Bible and in Jesus Christ. This is why we should accept God for who He is and put Him first in our lives.

But what happens if we reject a key or essential aspect of who God is?

Consider cheesecake as an example. Cheesecake is composed of cream cheese, sugar, and a graham cracker crust, among other things. If we leave the cream cheese out, it is not cheesecake. We would have a pretty poor concept of cheesecake if all we knew was cheesecake without cream cheese.

The God we believe in is not God if we deny an essential characteristic of who He is. And if our concept of Him is distorted, we relate to an idol of our own making rather than to the God of the Bible. Hosea 4:6 says, "My people are destroyed for lack of knowledge." So, denying part of who God is distorts or even destroys our relationship with God. We reject God Himself. If we deny that God created as described in Genesis, Exodus, and the rest of the Bible, we really deny an essential element of who God is.

The very first chapter of the Bible says God created in six days, and Exodus 20:11 says, "For in six days the LORD made the heavens and the earth, the sea, and all that is in them, and rested the seventh day." This Creation theme is carried throughout the entire Bible. And this tells us something about

God and His power, knowledge, and love.

God's power

The Bible tells us that God is all-powerful, all-knowing, and all-loving. There is nothing in Him that hindered Him from creating a wonderful world. And God Himself saw that it was good (Genesis 1:4, 10, 12, 18, 21, 25, 31).

Theistic evolution cannot hold that God is all-powerful, all-knowing, and all-loving at the same time. It can accept only two of these characteristics, at best, at any given time. To reject what the Bible says about creation is to reject important aspects of who God is. We would see Him as incapacitated in some way. That concept would change the way we think about God, and thus, it would affect our relationship with Him, just as the cheesecake without cream cheese would change what we thought about cheesecake.

The idea that God created over millions of years calls His power into question: God might be all-loving and all-knowing, but he just does not have so much power. He desired to fellowship with humans so much that he was willing to work with his limitations by taking millions of years to create them—millions of years of tooth and claw, pain, suffering, and death—so that finally he could create humankind! This certainly does not represent the God of the Bible. It changes our concept of God and, with it, our relationship with Him. When we do not take the Bible at face value, we create a god of our own making—a "designer god" or a god in our own image rather than us in the image of God.

God's knowledge

What does evolution imply about God's knowledge? It seems to say that although God is all-powerful and all-loving, he must not be very smart. This is why it took him millions of years to create us.

So again, we have a designer god who created through death by tooth and claw. So this god is limited by his knowledge but is making progress, doing the best he can under the circumstances. He is simply making it up as he goes, getting better and better as time goes on. He himself is in the process of evolution, like cell phones becoming better and better. Cell phones used to be huge pieces of equipment, but now they are smaller and more powerful. And we can use them not only for calling but also for texting, playing games, watching videos, and so much more. If we accept the idea of theistic evolution, we relate to a God who is himself in process, learning as he goes, hopefully getting better over time.

God's love

Finally, evolution does not allow for a God of love. A person may say that she loves her cell phone, but does her cell phone love her? Certainly not.

It is one thing if the cell phone does not love a person, but what if God does not love her? What if God really does not care whether he uses suffering and death as a means of creation? He is all-powerful and all-knowing but not a God who cares for his creatures, and so he is like a mad scientist, performing experiments on his creatures.

This would be the worst of all possibilities: a monster who experiments with life without consideration for his creatures! No wonder so many people choose to reject the idea of God. For evolution, God, if he exists at all, is impersonal.

A personal God

But the Bible also tells us that God is a personal God. This is the climax of the Creation account: God is personal. He created us in His image for fellowship. He gave us the Sabbath on the day He finished His work and rested as a day for special fellowship with Him. This is what sets the God of the Bible apart from all other gods.

God is a personal God who desires the fellowship of His creation. God was there with Adam and Eve on the evening of their creation. He did not wait millions and millions of years and then come down one day to say, "Oh, I forgot to tell you that I created you for fellowship!" This would make God have a combination of contradictory characteristics: he created humans for fellowship, yet he neglected to tell us for millions of years that we are his children. How could we relate to such a God?

Death before sin

The Bible makes it clear that the original creation was good. It was not tainted by sin or death. Theistic evolution states that death took place from the very beginning of life on Earth. In fact, the principle of survival of the fittest and death are the main mechanisms by which evolution is thought to take place. In this case, death is not the result of sin, as the Bible says; it is simply a natural result of the process of evolution.

And there are other theological issues with the theory of theistic evolution: sin itself.

The biblical meaning of *sin* is the transgression of the law. It is going against the character of God. It is the opposite of having a relationship with Him. It brings separation from God and, thus, death. Death is the result of sin, not of evolution.

By contrast, in the theory of evolution, there is no sin; we are getting better and better. And if there is no sin, then why the Cross? Why did Jesus have to die? If there is no such thing as sin, then there is no need for a Savior and no need for Jesus to die in our place.

This makes the Cross an accident of history rather than something in the plan of God even before creation (Revelation 13:8). In this way of thought, Jesus is not truly the Son of God. Evolution turns that which God gave as the ultimate manifestation of His love for us—the saving act of Christ on the cross—into foolishness and a false representation of who God is!

The Bible

Many people claim to accept the Bible as God's Word yet deny what it says about creation. To claim to accept the Bible as God's Word but deny what it says about creation is a contradiction. And this, in turn, calls into question the God who reveals Himself to us in the Bible.

Evolutionary thinking has led many to no longer regard the Bible as God's Word. It is seen as a fabrication of humankind—the passing on of legendary stories. The Bible is considered folk literature rather than the Word of God.

And if we are here by evolution over long ages, we ask the question again, Why did it take hundreds of millions of years for God to begin communicating with us through his spoken and written Word? And why did he wait until two thousand years ago to become one with us?

The nature of humankind

The theory of evolution raises another issue: Who are we? Was our ancestry carried on by natural selection from the primitive cell, through primitive life-forms, to more advanced forms of life, leading to primates and finally hominids? In other words, are we here because the basic principle of survival of the fittest guided our ancestry down to our generation? Are our origins explained and defined by the theory of evolution rather than by the creative power and plan of a loving God?

If so, what does this mean for who we are? Are we here by chance because a lightning strike and a concentration of chemicals coincided millions of years ago? That would mean we came from animals rather than from the hand of God.

And if this is the case, how should we then live? How should we relate to others? Does the principle of survival of the fittest provide the foundation for our moral lives? Does survival of the fittest become our Ten Commandments?

Mistaken ideas about the nature of life impact how we relate to God and how we treat each other. Hitler took evolution seriously as an explanation of origins. He saw the concept of survival of the fittest as the commandment by which we should live. Since, in his view, the Germanic peoples were superior to other human races, he thought it was their responsibility to dominate the world for the sake of evolutionary progress. His evolutionary view of the world resulted in the deaths of millions of people and misery for many more.

The Bible says that we were created by the hand of God in His image. We are sons and daughters of God, not the product of probability factors. Therefore, we should live in harmony with God's will, which is a totally different source of morality than that used by Hitler.

The Resurrection

What does theistic evolution mean for the resurrection of Jesus Christ? If God could not create by the word of his mouth, how could he resurrect Jesus Christ the way it is described in the Bible? Would it not take millions of years to re-evolve Christ?

And if it took God millions of years to create us, how can he resurrect us in "the twinkling of an eye" at the Second Coming (1 Corinthians 15:52)? Evolutionary thinking has led some theologians to conclude that there is no possibility of eternal life. This is a good life, they conclude. Live it to the full, for there is nothing after this!

The God of biblical creation and the god of evolution are two different gods. How could we worship a god who is in the process of evolution himself and was so incapacitated that he could only advance creation by tooth, claw, and death?

Evolutionary theory requires that we rewrite the history of God and, therefore, redefine His nature. In so doing, it leads to a relationship with a false god, an idol, rather than with the God of the Bible. How can we relate to the monster god of evolution? This is one reason why people are turning to agnosticism and atheism. They would prefer not to think about the existence of such a god.

When Christ appears the second time, He desires to return to a people who are waiting for Him as He has revealed Himself, not for some designer god. He will come for a people who are like Him in character rather than like designer gods who are the creations of our own imaginations.

Christ is coming for a people who are not in the dark about who He is. The Gospel of John says, "All things were made through Him" (John 1:3), yet Jesus condescended to become one with us. We have good news to proclaim! God is a God of love. He created us for fellowship with Himself. We are His sons and daughters! That completely changes the way we see and *know* God, the world, and others around us!

It is by virtue of creation that God is worthy of worship.

He is calling for a people who will come out of Babylon and "worship Him who made heaven and earth, the sea and springs of water" (Revelation 14:7). God is calling for a people who will proclaim the everlasting gospel, urging people to abandon their self-made gods and accept Jesus Christ as their personal Savior.

10

The Way, the Truth, and the Life

E. Edward Zinke and Bill Knott

The Gospel of John identifies seven "I AM" sayings from the preaching of Christ. The term *I AM* represents Deity, and its use goes back to the time of Abraham and Moses: "The LORD appeared to Abram and said to him, 'I am Almighty God' " (Genesis 17:1). "God said to Moses, 'I AM WHO I AM.' And He said, 'Thus you shall say to the children of Israel, "I AM has sent me to you" ' " (Exodus 3:14).

Moses, an Israelite, was adopted into the royal court by the daughter of Pharaoh, the king of Egypt. We are not told how long Moses remained at his Israelite home, but we do know that he was eventually raised and educated in Pharaoh's household. As a potential monarch of Egypt, Moses received the education of an Egyptian, both politically and religiously.

One day, after he had reached adulthood, he chanced upon an Egyptian who was unfairly and severely whipping an Israelite slave. Moses killed the abusive taskmaster and buried his body in the sand, hoping to keep the incident quiet. The next day, his secret was out. Fearing for his life, Moses fled into the wilderness, where he lived for forty years as a shepherd.

While in the wilderness, herding sheep for his father-in-law, Jethro, Moses came upon a burning bush that could not be extinguished. From the burning bush came a voice: "I AM WHO I AM" (verse 14). This was the voice of Deity. It was the same Deity who spoke to Abraham, Isaac, and Jacob.

The Old Testament God is the New Testament God

The Gospel of John picks up on this theme and shows the continuity of the Old Testament with the New Testament. The I AM statements from the New Testament are clearly linked with the I AM statements of the Old Testament.

Each of the I AM statements in John shows an action of Christ in relation to a miracle that He has just performed or will perform. They show the congruity of God's actions in the present with His actions in the past. We will show this by reviewing the first two I AM statements.

In the first I AM statement, "Jesus said to them, 'I am the bread of life' " (John 6:35). In this case, Jesus had fed the five thousand—fulfilling His claim as the Bread of Life. But the significance of His miracles went beyond that. After He fed the crowd, they quickly began to complain and then demand a miracle, as if they had not received one. They complained that Moses had provided manna and that Jesus should do the same.

In response to their grumbling, Jesus made it clear that Moses did not give them bread from heaven: "For the bread of God is He who comes down from heaven and gives life to the world" (verse 33). "This gave Jesus the opportunity to affirm two important truths: (1) it was not Moses who gave them the bread from heaven, but God (John 6:32; Ex. 16:15–16), and (2) the true bread from heaven, the bread that gives life to the world, is the one that the Father gives (John 6:33; cf. 1:14, 45;

5:39–40, 46), and those who receive it will never be hungry or thirsty again (6:35). This is truly a messianic claim."[1]

I AM the Light of the World

The second I AM statement is in John 8:12: "I am the light of the world." Included with this declaration is a promise: "He who follows Me shall not walk in darkness, but have the light of life" (verse 12). This linkage with light draws us back to Genesis 1 and the creation of light. John makes it clear that Jesus Christ is the same God who created light in the first place; He is both the Life-Giver and the Light. "All things were made through Him" (John 1:3), and "in Him was life, and the life was the light of men" (verse 4).

Strangely, the story now takes a sad turn. "And the light shines in the darkness, and the darkness did not comprehend it" (verse 5). "He was in the world, and though the world was made through him, the world did not recognize him. He came to that which was his own, but his own did not receive him" (verses 10, 11, NIV).

Rejecting the gospel is a recurring theme in the book of John. Those who ate of the bread with the five thousand rejected Christ because He did not fit their conception of the Messiah. Christ was rejected by many who observed the healing of the blind man, and many who saw the resurrection of Lazarus rejected Him because He did not fit their idea of the Messiah. The darkness did not comprehend the light.

The I AM statements

In the seven unambiguous I AM statements made by Jesus that are recorded in John's Gospel, He consciously and intentionally applied the sacred name of God, revealed in the Torah, to Himself. Historians of intertestamental Judaism and first-century Judaism remind us that no Jew would ever take upon his lips the formulation of "I AM." This name belonged only to God, who identified Himself to Moses at the burning bush: "I am the God of your father, the God of Abraham, the God of Isaac and the God of Jacob" (Exodus 3:6, NIV). "God said to Moses, 'I AM WHO I AM. This is what you are to say to the Israelites: "I AM has sent me to you" ' " (verse 14, NIV).

Yet Jesus did not hesitate to take the most sacred name in Judaism and apply it to Himself. In seven deliberate statements, He expressly identified Himself with the Trinity and with the God whom, for centuries, the Israelites had declared to be their unique and all-powerful Deity:

1. "I am the bread of life" (John 6:35, 41, 48, 51).
2. "I am the light of the world" (John 8:12; 9:5).
3. "I am the door" (John 10:7, 9).
4. "I am the good shepherd" (verses 11, 14).
5. "I am the resurrection and the life" (John 11:25).
6. "I am the way, the truth, and the life" (John 14:6).
7. "I am the true vine" (John 15:1, 5).

As if anticipating the arguments of those who would later try to separate Jesus from His claim of divinity, He employed these vivid metaphors and added explicit declarations of His role as the God of the Old Testament: " 'Very truly I tell you,' Jesus answered, 'before Abraham was born, I am!' " (John 8:58, NIV). His hearers were in no doubt about His claims to divinity. The biblical record says that "they took up stones to throw at Him" for blasphemy (verse 59).

Jesus likewise invoked the sacred name to identify Himself when the mob came to arrest Him in the Garden of Gethsemane. His declaration has an instantaneous effect: "When

Jesus said, 'I am he,' they drew back and fell to the ground" (John 18:6, NIV).

In dozens of other direct citations of the Old Testament and clear allusions to Old Testament passages, John recounts the story of Jesus as a specific fulfillment of the predictions made by the Old Testament prophets. In Psalm 22, David prophesied about the Messiah, "They divide my clothes among them and cast lots for my garment" (verse 18, NIV). John identifies this event as a prophecy directly fulfilled in the manner of Christ's crucifixion:

> They [the Roman soldiers] said therefore among themselves, "Let us not tear it, but cast lots for it, whose it shall be," that the Scripture might be fulfilled which says:
>
> > "They divided My garments among them,
> > And for My clothing they cast lots."
>
> Therefore the soldiers did these things (John 19:24).

John links multiple aspects of the story of Jesus' supreme sacrifice to the prophecies of the Old Testament, anchoring his witness to Jesus in both history and prophecy:

- Jesus is betrayed by one of His own (Psalm 41:9).
- His clothing is divided as predicted (Psalm 22:18).
- None of His bones are broken (Numbers 9:12).
- He is offered gall to drink (Psalm 69:21).
- He is hated without cause (verse 4).

The sheer volume and specificity of John's citations and allusions to the Old Testament irrevocably link his witness to

Jesus with the witness of the sages and prophets of the previous four thousand years of human history. John's work is, in the fullest sense, a persuasive work: "These are written that you may believe that Jesus is the Christ, the Son of God, and that by believing you may have life in his name" (John 20:31, NIV). Indeed, believing—faith founded in the trust that God's revelation of Himself in the Old Testament has come to full expression in the life and ministry of Jesus of Nazareth—is referenced more than ninety times in John's Gospel.

The totality of John's writing about Jesus associates Him with every period of human history: the creation of the earth, the witness of the Old Testament to the coming Messiah, the Savior's life that John witnessed as a companion to Jesus, John's witness to the truth of Jesus' saving death and resurrection, and the future resolution of the problem of evil through the eternal ministry of Jesus, as seen in the book of Revelation.

And what do the I AM statements mean for the lived experience of humans? They simply deliver on the deep yearning of every heart—the desire for life and liberty. That is how God created us, and that is why these declarations move us today. "You shall know the truth, and the truth shall make you free" (John 8:32).

Modern thinking sees truth as transient and indeterminate, but the Gospel of John declares that Jesus Christ, the Word, and the Word made flesh, is the truth we seek. And when we claim Him as our Savior, we enjoy the freedom our hearts long for.

---

1. Ángel Manuel Rodríguez, ed., *Andrews Bible Commentary*, vol. 2, *New Testament* (Berrien Springs, MI: Andrews University Press, 2022), 1430.

11

The Father, the Son, and the Spirit

Jiří Moskala

John 13–17 focuses on the farewell discourse of Jesus and the concept of the Trinity. This is a significant topic because it reveals the nature, purpose, work, and function of different Persons within the Holy Trinity. It also describes Their mutual relationship. The unity between the Father and the Son is a model that we can emulate as we seek a close relationship with our Savior, Jesus Christ.

The Triune God is engaged in our salvation and life. It is important for us to understand God's revelation about Himself because only then can we comprehend Him better and relate to the Godhead in a proper way. He is the Creator of the universe and the Author of the plan of redemption. Appreciating this will help us serve Him more meaningfully and worship Him out of gratitude for our salvation (John 1:1, 2; Colossians 1:16, 17; Hebrews 11:3).

The Lord is One

The fundamental mystery of the Christian faith is the belief in the Triune God. As Seventh-day Adventists, we confess that God is One but manifested in Three distinct Persons—namely, the Father, the Son, and the Holy Spirit. When we speak about God, we need to remember that we enter holy ground, and we need to do so in deep humility, knowing our limits. We are using imperfect human language to describe an Infinite God! The transcendent God always surpasses even our finest categories of thinking and logic. The best attitude in such a situation is the humility to which God invited Moses at the burning bush: "Take off your sandals, for the place where you are standing is holy ground" (Exodus 3:5, NIV). We need to realize that we know God only because He has made Himself known to us. What we perceive about Him was revealed to us; we are totally dependent upon His self-revelation (Exodus 34:6, 7; Deuteronomy 29:29). Thus, our only correct response to His Word is to carefully listen, eagerly learn, and wholeheartedly obey (Isaiah 66:2).

The basic confession of faith in the Hebrew Bible—"Hear, O Israel: The LORD our God, the LORD is one" (Deuteronomy 6:4)—is a clear proclamation of monotheism, which Jesus affirmed (Mark 12:29). Called the Shema, this declaration announces God as being One in a very fundamental and unequivocal statement. This oneness of God is stressed several times in the rest of the Bible because He alone is the true God and there is none beside Him (Deuteronomy 4:35, 39; Nehemiah 9:6; Psalm 86:10; Isaiah 44:6; Zechariah 14:9). It is important to note that the New Testament's authors also proclaimed that God is One, and thus they did not see this announcement as a contradiction of the Trinitarian thinking to which they adhered (Matthew 28:19; 2 Corinthians 13:14).

Abiding in Jesus

The Gospel according to John invites readers to follow the story of Jesus by believing and abiding in Him. The center of our faith is Jesus Christ. True religion is rooted in Jesus. To believe in Jesus is one of the principal thoughts in John. The verb meaning *to believe* occurs ninety-eight times in the Greek version of John's Gospel. It is significant that the nouns translated *faith* and *belief* do not appear in this Gospel, which means that John is emphasizing the importance of having a vital and active faith in Jesus to trust Him. Maintaining a relationship is an action; it is not static. In John 15, Jesus especially stresses how His followers need to abide or stay rooted in Him.

In His relationships with the Father and the Holy Spirit, Jesus was not working in isolation from the Triune God. In this Gospel, He is closely associated with His Father. To His disciples, He revealed His relationship to the Father as well as the special role and function of the Third Person of the Trinity—the Holy Spirit. Jesus stated that it was to the disciples' advantage that the presence of the Holy Spirit replace Him, for the Spirit would be everywhere and guide them into the whole truth (John 16:7, 8).

Seven main facts must be stressed:

1. The primary premise and the entry point to understanding glimpses of our transcendent Triune God is accepting the divinity of Jesus Christ. Jesus Christ is God. This truth is attested in the beginning, at the end, and throughout the Gospel of John. In the Gospel's introduction, John states that Jesus is (a) eternal, (b) united with the Father, (c) God, (d) a distinct Person from His Father, and (e) the Creator: "In the beginning was the Word, and the Word was with God, and the Word was God. He was in the beginning with God. All things were made through him, and without him was not any

thing made that was made" (John 1:1–3, ESV). In John 1:1, the word *was*, from the Greek term *ēn*, which is an imperfect of the verb *eimi,* refers to a continuous time. So this means if one can imagine a beginning, in that beginning, Jesus was already in existence.

There was never a time when Jesus was not (Isaiah 9:6; Micah 5:2). At the conclusion of the Gospel is Thomas's beautiful confession about Jesus: "My Lord and my God!" (John 20:28).

2. Christ's radical assertions testify to His divinity. Jesus Christ's claims were so profound that there are only two possibilities: either He was God, or He was a madman and a deceiver. Consider Jesus' own testimony:

- "You believe in God, believe also in Me" (John 14:1).
- "I am the resurrection and the life. He who believes in Me, though he may die, he shall live" (John 11:25).
- "The Father judges no one, but has entrusted all judgment to the Son" (John 5:22, NIV).
- "I am the bread of life" (John 6:35).
- "I am the living bread which came down from heaven. If anyone eats of this bread, he will live forever" (verse 51).
- "I am the light of the world. Whoever follows me will never walk in darkness" (John 8:12, NIV).
- "This is the will of the Father who sent Me, that of all He has given Me I should lose nothing, but should raise it up at the last day" (John 6:39).
- "I am the way, the truth, and the life. No one comes to the Father except through Me" (John 14:6).
- "He who has seen Me has seen the Father" (verse 9).
- "All should honor the Son just as they honor the Father. He who does not honor the Son does not honor the Father who sent Him" (John 5:23).

- "I have come down from heaven" (John 6:38).
- "I and My Father are one" (John 10:30).
- "Before Abraham was, I AM!" (John 8:58).

The Jews wanted to stone Him for this blasphemy (verse 59). In addition, Jesus claimed to have the power to forgive sins (Luke 5:24), and He accepted adoration when people worshiped Him (John 9:38). He called His disciples to follow Him (Matthew 4:19; 8:22; 9:9; 10:38; 16:24) and declared: "Come to Me, all you who labor and are heavy laden, and I will give you rest" (Matthew 11:28).

Ellen G. White explains the importance of accepting the divinity of Jesus with the following powerful words: "If men reject the testimony of the inspired Scriptures concerning the deity of Christ, it is in vain to argue the point with them; for no argument, however conclusive, could convince them. 'The natural man receiveth not the things of the Spirit of God: for they are foolishness unto him: neither can he know them, because they are spiritually discerned.' 1 Corinthians 2:14. None who hold this error can have a true conception of the character or the mission of Christ, or of the great plan of God for man's redemption."[1]

3. Jesus is the Creator. The Word has created all things (John 1:3). Because Jesus has created all things, He Himself is not created but the Creator (Colossians 1:16). Through the Son, God created the world, and the Son is the Sustainer and the exact representation of the Father (Hebrews 1:2, 3).

4. Jesus has life inherent in Himself. He is the Source of life; not only does He give life, but He is life (John 1:4; 5:26). He can lay down His life and can take it again (see John 10:17, 18). He is able to give life to us; He is the resurrection, "the way, the truth, and the life" (John 11:25; 14:6). Eternal life

is always dependent on Jesus (John 3:36; 6:40; 10:28; 1 John 5:11–13). Only He can set people free from the bondage of sin; His truth sets people free (John 8:32).

5. Jesus Christ came to reveal His Father. John declares that He interpreted and explained to people who God is. He revealed God perfectly because He came from Him. Jesus speaks frequently about the Living God as His Father and reveals His close connection with Him. The word translated *Father* occurs 121 times in the Greek version of John.

6. Jesus was equal to and one with His Father (John 10:30). He does everything in harmony with His Father (John 5:30; 7:16; 10:38; 14:10). No one can come to the Father but through Him (see John 14:6). Jesus is the Son of God (Luke 3:38; John 11:27; 1 John 5:12), who reveals the Father (John 1:18; 14:6–9), and is always One with the Father (John 10:29–36).

The Jews correctly understood Jesus' statement that He considered Himself to be God and attempted to arrest Him (verses 33, 39). On another occasion, when Jesus healed an invalid on the Sabbath and the Jews accused Him of transgressing the Sabbath commandment, Jesus stated: "My Father is working until now, and I am working" (John 5:17, ESV). John commented on this situation: "Therefore the Jews sought all the more to kill Him, because He not only broke the Sabbath, but also said that God was His Father, making Himself equal with God" (verse 18).

Also, the apostle Paul preached that Jesus was the Messiah, the Son of God (Acts 9:20, 22). The title "Son of God" designates a Divine Person who was sent by the Almighty God to be the Messiah as the fulfillment of Old Testament promises of redemption beginning with Genesis 3:15. This title should not be understood in the literal sense of birth but as a divine epithet that refers to Him as the Messiah, having a unique relationship with the Lord and the mission to save humanity. The Gospels were written to testify that Jesus of Nazareth was that promised Son of God (Mark 1:1; Luke 1:35; 3:38; John 20:31).

The whole picture is crystal clear. Jesus Christ is God: He is our Creator (John 1:1–3; Colossians 1:16), Savior (John 12:32; Acts 4:10–12), Judge (John 5:24–30), Intercessor (Romans 8:34; Hebrews 7:25), King (Matthew 25:34; Revelation 17:14), Lord (John 13:13, 14), and Friend (John 15:14).

7. The Gospel according to John gives the best explanation of the role of the Holy Spirit. The person and work of the Holy Spirit is revealed by Jesus Himself in a transparent manner. Jesus speaks about Him as the One who converts people to God (John 16:8–10, 13) and names Him as another "Comforter" (John 14:16, 26; 15:26; 16:7, KJV) who also is called "the Spirit of truth" (John 14:17; 15:26; 16:13). He will teach Christians all things and remind them of everything that Christ told His disciples (see John 14:26). He will guide Christ's followers into "all truth" (John 16:13). He comes from the Father as well as from the Son (John 14:26; 15:26). He will teach believers more about Christ (John 15:26) and glorify Him (John 16:14). "He will convict the world concerning sin and righteousness and judgment" (verses 8, 9, ESV). He will also reveal future events (verse 13).

In summary, God's love is true and unselfish love. This is why He speaks in the plural form of *We* (Genesis 1:26; 3:22; 11:7; Isaiah 6:8). God is in fellowship within Himself; He is community. He is in a relationship with the Godhead and also with His creation. The community of God is the source and basis for all other communities within His creation, including relationships within humanity. The pattern of love, unity, and work within the Trinity is the fountain from which springs all true relationships. Our God longs for meaningful relationships with people because He is not a solitary Person. He did not create humans to live in isolation but to enjoy social life in marriage and community.

An open heart brings understanding

The unity between the Father and the Son in working for our salvation is stunning, and the sustaining work of the Holy Spirit is breathtaking. The Holy Spirit is close to humanity. He communicates with us and encourages us to know God and follow His teaching faithfully. Only because of His presence in our lives can we resist evil, obey God, and grow in the grace of Christ. He is the best Comforter in times of disappointment, distress, despair, hurt, depression, misunderstanding, suffering, and persecution. We need to open our hearts to God and respond to the promptings of the Spirit in order to love, obey, and worship the Triune God.

Our finite minds are unable to understand the magnificence, sovereignty, and grandiosity of the Triune God. He transcends our limited capacities and our feeble attempts to comprehend Him. We can only stand in awe as we marvel at His revelation of Himself.

We need to be careful—extremely careful—in our attempts to explain God and avoid creating Him in our image! Humans were created in His image, not vice versa. In view of the uniqueness and otherness of our God, it becomes clear that we cannot grasp the full picture of our Lord, as He is above our logical categorizations. We can only ask for a glimpse, for a wonder, to see Him, worship Him, and serve our awesome God who surpasses our concepts of knowledge and judgment (Exodus 33:18, 19; 34:6, 7). He is always above all things.

Instead of trying to explain God, let us relate to Him personally as our Lord and Savior. As we grow closer to Him, we will lovingly fellowship with others, walking faithfully with those who are part of His marvelous creation.

---

1. Ellen G. White, *The Great Controversy* (Mountain View, CA: Pacific Press®, 1950), 524.

12

The Hour of Glory: The Cross and Resurrection

Anthony Kent

During the platinum jubilee of Queen Elizabeth II, an amazing story emerged. The queen was walking outside the grounds of Balmoral Castle in Scotland. She was wearing casual clothes and was attended by only one security officer, Richard Griffin, who was also dressed informally. Along a remote path, they met two tourists from America who were on a walking vacation in Britain. The queen paused to say hello and chat with the travelers. Amazingly, the tourists did not recognize the queen, who was probably one of the most photographed people on the planet.[1]

As they conversed for some minutes, the Americans shared where they lived and where they were going on their vacation. They asked the unrecognized queen where she lived, and she said she lived in London but traveled up to her holiday home nearby. When asked how long she had been visiting the area, the queen responded that she had been coming to the area for over eighty years. She was then asked by the tourists whether, during all those visits to the area, she had ever met the queen.

Most likely with a twinkle in her eye, the queen responded that Richard, her companion, meets with the queen. The travelers were thrilled! They wanted to have their picture taken with Richard because he knew the queen. They handed the queen their camera and asked her to be the photographer.

After the picture had been taken, Richard—in an act of kindness to assuage the foreigners' future feelings of embarrassment—then offered to change places with the queen, who was still unrecognized by the couple, so that a photo could be taken of the tourists with the queen. They parted, still unaware that they had been looking at, talking with, and sharing photographs with Queen Elizabeth II, who was the longest-reigning monarch in the history of Britain.[2]

No doubt, at some point after their experience with the queen, those two travelers—perhaps when they looked closely at their vacation pictures—realized that they had been in the presence of royalty.

Pilate and Jesus

Pontius Pilate met with Jesus, but he missed the opportunity to recognize Jesus' identity. William Barclay, writing about that meeting between Jesus and Pilate, recorded in John 18:28–19:16, observes, "No one can read this story without seeing the sheer majesty of Jesus."[3] It seems that Pilate was the exception. While it is unlikely that Pilate ever read John's Gospel, he *lived* through this experience and did not recognize "the sheer majesty of Jesus." John's readers have known Jesus' true identity as the "Word" since the opening words of the Gospel: "In the beginning was the Word, and the Word was with God, and the Word was God. He was in the beginning with God. All things were made through him, and without him was not any thing made that was made" (John 1:1–3).[4]

Further, in John 1:14, Jesus, the Word, is described as "*full* of grace and truth" (emphasis added). Jesus is also described as "the true light" (verse 9). "Grace and truth came through Jesus Christ" (verse 17). And in this first chapter of John's Gospel, there is the predictive comment: "He [Jesus] was in the world, and the world was made through him, yet the world did not know him" (verse 10). Clearly, Pilate did not know Him; perhaps Pilate did not care to know Him.

Several commentators make the point that in John's description of the meeting between Pilate and Jesus, there are only two people in the room—Jesus and Pilate. One commentator writes, "At this moment all the other actors in the passion disappear from the scene."[5] Another observes, "Moreover, an equestrian procurator such as Pilate in an insignificant province such as Judea had no assistants of high rank who could help him carry out his administrative and judicial duties."[6] Yet another commentator notes that John has a convention, similar to other biblical writers, "to reduce powerful scenes to two main figures."[7] In this case, it is Jesus and Pilate.

Ellen G. White writes that initially, "Pilate looked upon Him with no friendly eyes."[8] John's account says that Pilate "called" Jesus. This is not the call of David unto the Lord: "In my distress I called upon the LORD" (Psalm 18:6). Rather, this call of Pilate was of the arrogant to one he deemed subordinate, as a master would summon his slave.

The interrogation

The location where Pilate interrogated Jesus is also important because it reveals the power dynamic of this whole episode. John specifically states it occurred at the governor's Jerusalem headquarters—the *praetorium* (John 18:33). This was Pilate's residence when he was in Jerusalem. He was normally based in Caesarea Maritima on the Mediterranean coast. Pilate, as a Gentile, made no provision to remove yeast or leaven from his home or diet in anticipation of the Passover. The Jewish leaders, the prosecutors of Jesus, were careful not to enter the residence of Pilate "so that they would not be defiled, but could eat the Passover" (verse 28). Jesus, as a Jew, was not a recipient of this courtesy. The Roman Pilate, "an ethnocentric colonialist governor,"[9] was known to be spiteful and cruel toward the Jews, with many being unjustly executed, their finances plundered, and their laws of idolatry deliberately breached. However, in this specific example, he respectfully deferred to Jewish sensitivities. He was the one who left his residence to meet with the Jewish leadership outside of his residence, where they would not be contaminated by his unclean house. According to John's record, seven times Pilate "moves between the Jewish chief priests waiting outside and Jesus inside the *praetorium*."[10] Although "Pilate possessed *imperium* or supreme magisterial power in the region,"[11] in this episode, he was very submissive to the Jewish leaders.

John is also most likely making a subtle point about the status of Jesus. No accusation, yeast, or, indeed, any external element that could be imposed upon Jesus would ever pollute the pure Lamb of God. Though flesh—in the unclean *praetorium* within a polluted world—Jesus is sinless, the Light of the world (John 8:12); He unfalteringly remains "full of grace and truth" (John 1:14).

After conferring outside with the Jewish leaders, Pilate returned to his residence for the inquisition of Jesus. His first question to Jesus was loaded with irony and disdain: "Are you the King of the Jews?" (John 18:33). Pilate could scarcely believe the credibility of the charge against Jesus. His question was "emphatically scornful."[12] Are *you* the King of the Jews?

No army of rebellion was in sight; it was inconceivable that the Galilean peasant was a threat to Rome or anyone.

Jesus cares for Pilate

Jesus' response to Pilate's question was intelligent, measured, and even pastoral toward His interrogator. Jesus effectively asked Pilate, Is this your own personal question or a question from others? Of course, Jesus knew the answer to His question to Pilate even before He asked it, but He asked it of Pilate to reach the heart of the Roman governor. Ellen G. White offers this important insight: Jesus "knew that the Holy Spirit was striving with Pilate."[13] Even when being examined by Pilate, who is neither "a just nor a conscientious judge,"[14] Jesus was concerned with the Roman's salvation and His love for him was evident. In this setting, Jesus demonstrated the same love for Pilate as He did when He was being crucified, and He prayed, "Father, forgive them, for they know not what they do" (Luke 23:34).

Ellen G. White also observes that during Pilate's judgment of Jesus, Pilate's "gaze rested searchingly on Jesus. He had had to deal with all kinds of criminals; but never before had a man bearing marks of such goodness and nobility been brought before him. On His face he saw no sign of guilt, no expression of fear, no boldness or defiance. He saw a man of calm and dignified bearing, whose countenance bore not the marks of a criminal, but the signature of heaven."[15]

She further describes what happened in Pilate's heart at this moment: "Pilate understood Christ's meaning; but pride arose in his heart. He would not acknowledge the conviction that pressed upon him."[16]

Pilate's retort was, "Am I a Jew?" (John 18:35). His answer was clear and unambiguous: No! He was not a Jew, and no, he was not interested in the beckoning of the Holy Spirit and Jesus. He would not allow his heart to be moved.

Will Pilate listen?

But Pilate was curious and had more questions for Jesus: "Why do your own people, your own religious leaders, want you executed? What have you done?" (verse 35, author's translation). Jesus then shared with Pilate what ultimately becomes an essential point of John's Gospel: "My kingdom is not of this world. If my kingdom were of this world, my servants would have been fighting, that I might not be delivered over to the Jews. But my kingdom is not from the world" (verse 36).

Pilate latched onto a seeming admission from Jesus: " 'So you are a king?' Jesus answered, 'You say that I am a king. For this purpose I was born and for this purpose I have come into the world—to bear witness to the truth. Everyone who is of the truth listens to my voice' " (verse 37).

Jesus' gentle but earnest urging upon the heart of this ruthless official of the iron empire of Rome is clear. Readers of John can readily perceive exactly what Jesus is doing here. They have seen it before. When Jesus had met with curious individuals, such as Nicodemus (John 3:1–15) and the Samaritan woman at the well (John 4:5–41), they listened to the truth of Jesus, opened their hearts to Him, and ultimately their lives were positively transformed. This is verified in John 19 when John describes that same Nicodemus—a Jewish religious leader who had chosen not to condemn Jesus to crucifixion—as bringing an expensive mixture of myrrh and aloes, at great personal risk, to prepare the deceased body of Jesus for burial (John 19:39).

Will Pilate listen to the truth like Nicodemus or the woman

at the well? Will he open his heart to grace and eternal life? He is in an exceptionally privileged position; he is in a room alone with Jesus, the Christ, the Messiah. Emmanuel is in the flesh, pleading with him. In this setting, Jesus reveals His amazing love for people—all people, even Pilate, who is known by his contemporaries for "venality, violence, thefts, assaults, abusive behavior, frequent executions of untried prisoners, and his endless savage ferocity."[17]

What does Pilate do with this opportunity to accept the truth of Jesus and eternal life? Filled with arrogant pride, he tersely dismisses the gracious appeal of Jesus and incredulously blurts, "What is truth?" (John 18:38).

The irony of Pilate's response with this question—"What is truth?"—is extraordinary. Pilate is alone in a room with Jesus. Jesus is truth and grace. Pilate is looking at Truth, speaking with Truth, and hearing Truth, yet he chooses not to recognize Truth—the Truth standing before him in an otherwise empty room. Pilate is alone with the Light of the world, but he chooses not to see the Light. Pilate's failure to recognize the identity of Jesus is not a simple matter of visual recognition, like that of the tourists who did not recognize Queen Elizabeth in an unexpected context.

Pilate can see, hear, and comprehend the Truth all too well, but he chooses to reject Him. History records Pilate's many flaws and faults, but he is never characterized as dull or dim. This is a deliberate choice. "The majesty of Jesus never shone more radiantly than in the hour when he was on trial before the world."[18] Pilate does not just have a front-row seat during this trial of Jesus; he has a private audience with the radiant and majestic Jesus.

Pilate ensures that Jesus has no opportunity to answer his question of "What is truth?" He immediately leaves the room and goes outside to the Jewish leaders. The imagery of Pilate's departure evokes that of Judas Iscariot from the room of the Last Supper to betray Jesus (John 13:30). Just as Judas ultimately confesses the innocence of Jesus (Matthew 27:3, 4), Pilate is convinced that Jesus is innocent of all charges (John 18:38; 19:4, 6).

Pilate believed in the innocence of Jesus. He made repeated attempts to save Jesus from the cross. He was even willing to acknowledge Jesus as king—"the King of the Jews" (John 19:19). But tragically, he was unwilling to accept Jesus as *his* King and Savior.

Career over Christ

In 1961, an Italian archaeological team working at Caesarea Maritima, where Pilate was based as governor from AD 26 to AD 36, discovered a damaged Latin stone inscription from the time of his rulership. An idiomatically reconstructed translation of the inscription reads: "Pontius Pilate, prefect of Judea, has given (or has dedicated) to the people of Caesarea a public building (or temple) in honor of Tiberius."[19] If this stone inscription is to be believed, it seems that Pilate's heart was dedicated to the Roman emperor Tiberius rather than to Jesus.

If only he had acknowledged the Truth!

Pilate was dedicated to being positively regarded by his superiors in Rome. In his world, this was the path to wealth, power, and an elevated position. To achieve this ambition, he needed to rule Judea with excellence. Surprisingly, he had limited military resources to impose Roman power on Judea—a notoriously difficult region to govern—so when it suited his purposes, he would appease the Jewish leadership. His addiction to ambition made him vulnerable to manipulative power brokers. Pilate was astute enough to recognize that his selfish agenda would not be propelled by Jesus and His kingdom—and acceptance of Jesus' kingdom would reverse Pilate's desired trajectory. Though Jesus was innocent, He was expendable. Jesus willingly died as Pilate's Savior, but Pilate chose to use Jesus' execution as a mere means to advance his career. It was a tragic decision.

---

1. James Clifford Kent, "Queen Elizabeth II: Capturing the World's Most Photographed Woman in Life and Death," *The Conversation*, September 19, 2022, https://theconversation.com/queen-elizabeth-ii-capturing-the-worlds-most-photographed-woman-in-life-and-death-190490.

2. Henry Jones, "Former Protection Officer Recounts Moment Tourists Did Not Recognise Queen," *Independent*, June 3, 2022, https://www.independent.co.uk/news/uk/american-royal-sky-news-her-majesty-platinum-jubilee-b2093534.html.

3. William Barclay, *The Gospel of John*, New Daily Study Bible (Louisville, KY: Westminster John Knox, 2001), 2:283.

4. Unless otherwise noted, all Scripture quotations in this chapter are from the Holy Bible, English Standard Version®.

5. Leon Morris, *The Gospel According to John*, rev. ed., New International Commentary on the New Testament (Grand Rapids, MI: Eerdmans, 1995), 678.

6. Andreas J. Köstenberger, *John*, Baker Exegetical Commentary on the New Testament (Grand Rapids, MI: Baker Academic, 2004), 526.

7. Helen K. Bond, "Pilate, Pontius," in *The New Interpreter's Dictionary of the Bible*, vol. 4 (Nashville, TN: Abingdon, 2009), 527.

8. Ellen G. White, *The Desire of Ages* (Mountain View, CA: Pacific Press®, 1940), 723.

9. Craig S. Keener, *The Gospel of John: A Commentary* (Peabody, MA: Hendrickson, 2003), 2:1105.

10. Bond, "Pilate, Pontius," 527; emphasis in the original.

11. Bond, 526.

12. Köstenberger, *John*, 527.

13. White, *Desire of Ages*, 726, 727.

14. Ellen G. White, "Jewish Hatred," *Advent Review and Sabbath Herald*, November 7, 1899, 1.

15. White, *Desire of Ages*, 724.
16. White, 727.
17. Bond, "Pilate, Pontius," 526.
18. Barclay, 2:283, 284.
19. James J. C. Cox, "Pontius Pilate and the Caesarea Inscription: Archeology Supplies Corroborative Evidence," *Ministry*, April 1975, 12.

13

Epilogue: Knowing Jesus and His Word

Anthony Kent

Towering above the blue waters of the Gulf of Naples is Mount Vesuvius. From its 4,203-foot summit, there are gorgeous views of the Italian coast, including Naples, Sorrento, and the picturesque island of Capri. Vesuvius, still an active volcano, is best known for the devastating eruption in the autumn of AD 79 that destroyed Pompeii, Herculaneum, Stabiae, Torre Annunziata, and other settlements, villages, and communities in just a few hours.

In the fall of AD 79, people were still rebuilding from a major earthquake that had struck in AD 62. It was clear a mere four days before Vesuvius erupted that all was not normal. There were continuous earth tremors; wells known for plentiful supplies of cool, refreshing water were dry; and steam was hissing from cracks in the ground. Tragically, people did not evacuate.

During the eruption, it is estimated that gas, ash, and stones were propelled to an extraordinary height of more than nineteen miles. Most likely tens of thousands of people lost their lives in the calamity.

Remarkably, only a single eyewitness records this massive seismic tragedy: Pliny the Younger.[1] In two letters to the Roman historian Tacitus, Pliny the Younger describes the enormous mushroom cloud, the debris falling from the sky, its rapid accumulation on the ground, and people resorting to fastening pillows to their heads as they attempted to flee. He notes the complete darkness—darker than any night—even though the eruption was during daylight hours. Most disturbingly, he writes of the surging masses running for their lives, slowed by the sheer number of men, women, and screaming children. The odor of sulfur, the flames, and the heaving repeated earthquakes, together with a vivid description of what could only be a tsunami, all feature in his record. Pliny also portrays the vastness of the area covered by the cloud: "It girdled [the distant] Capri and made it vanish, it hid Misenum's promontory."[2]

Being a well-populated region, surely the enormity of the spectacle, the loudness, and the tragic fatalities must have attracted the attention of throngs. But of those who succeeded in escaping, the only recorder was Pliny the Younger?

From our twenty-first-century perspective—where billions of people routinely carry cell phones equipped with cameras capable of immediately uploading any event, important or unimportant, to the internet for global viewing—this is astonishing. Yet, to be fair to those living in the vicinity of Vesuvius, very few events in antiquity, even significant episodes, were recorded by those who were eyewitnesses to specific incidents.

The witness

Just as Pliny the Younger stands in history as a witness to the mighty eruption, John, the beloved disciple, is a witness to something significantly greater than the world's most famous volcanic event. John is a witness of the ministry of Jesus Christ, the Son of God. And John is not alone. There are other credible witnesses, such as Matthew, Mark, and Luke. Luke tells his readers that "many have undertaken to compile a narrative of the things that have been accomplished among us" (Luke 1:1).[3] In the context of antiquity, the number of reliable records detailing the life of Jesus is amazing. The quantity and thoroughness of these records highlight the significance of Jesus.

John was obsessed with being a witness. In the English Standard Version (ESV) translation, the word *witness* features twenty-nine times in John's Gospel. In Matthew and Mark, *witness* appears only four times in each; in Luke, the word occurs just twice. Clearly, *witness* and being a witness are priorities for John.

The truth is also important for John. Once again, this is typified in his vocabulary. The word *truth* is found twenty-six times in the ESV translation of the fourth Gospel. No other book in the Bible uses this word more frequently than the Gospel of John. The book that uses *truth* the next most frequently is Psalms, which is a considerably larger volume than John, yet it uses *truth* only ten times. The three epistles of John use that same word a total of twenty times. It is clear from the repeated usage that truth matters to John. Being a witness is important to John, but he also wants to be a truthful witness—he wants to reveal the truth.

But John is not a witness to trumpet his own importance. He is not interested in receiving any accolades or riding a wave of fame that may result in personal benefits. To identify himself as a witness or as having been present at an event, John typically refers to himself discreetly in the third person. Sometimes he styles himself as "another disciple" (John 18:15), "that disciple" (verse 15), or "the other disciple" (verse 16; John 20:8), and once he uses "the sons of Zebedee" (John 21:2), which obviously includes himself and his brother James. On other occasions, he describes himself as "one of his disciples, whom Jesus loved" (John 13:23); "the disciple whom he [Jesus] loved" (John 19:26); "the other disciple, the one whom Jesus loved" (John 20:2); "that disciple whom Jesus loved" (John 21:7); and "the disciple whom Jesus loved" (verse 20).

If Jesus loved me, He can love you

When John calls himself "the disciple whom Jesus loved," he does so not to highlight his own attributes but the virtues of Jesus. Jesus is the loving One rather than John being the lovable one.

Readers of the New Testament are well aware that John had some rather unlovable traits. He had a temper like thunder (Mark 3:17), probably smelled like fish (Luke 5:2, 10), wanted to call down deadly fire from heaven on some unsuspecting Samaritans (Luke 9:52–54), and with his manipulative mother, was embarrassingly ambitious for a prestigious position (Matthew 20:20, 21). Yet Jesus did love John and transformed him into a self-effacing, loving, and lovable disciple.

This love that Jesus has for John is not an exclusive love. John shows Jesus to have love and a fond regard for all people. This same author writes what are perhaps the best-known portions of Scripture: "For God so loved the world . . ." (John 3:16), and "God is love" (1 John 4:8). John's simple but profound articulation of God's love, together with his miraculous transformation by Jesus, encourages readers of his Gospel to contemplate: *If Jesus can love someone like John with those character flaws, He can love me. And if the Lord can transform John, He can transform me too.*

Experiencing Jesus

John's emphasis on witness comes to the fore with the concluding chapter of the book—John 21. This is an epilogue with purpose. He wants his readers to know Jesus—not just know *about* Jesus but *experience* Jesus. John had experienced Jesus. He had been wonderfully transformed by Jesus and is eager for all to have that same experience.

The final verses of the previous chapter set the scene: "Now Jesus did many other signs in the presence of the disciples, which are not written in this book; but these are written so that you may believe that Jesus is the Christ, the Son of God, and that by believing you may have life in his name" (John 20:30, 31).

John's whole purpose in writing this Gospel is not just to provide a historical record of an important event, like the eruption of Mount Vesuvius, or evidence for an intellectual belief in Jesus. Rather, John wants his readers to believe that Jesus is the Christ, the Son of God, and that they will have life—eternal life, an enhanced life—in His name.

The opening words of John 21 are significant: "After this Jesus revealed himself again to the disciples by the Sea of Tiberias, and he revealed himself in this way" (verse 1). The Greek word translated as "revealed" means "to cause to become visible, reveal, expose publicly."[4] John uses similar language in one of his other books—Revelation, "the revelation of Jesus Christ" (Revelation 1:1). The Greek word used in Revelation 1:1 means "making fully known, revelation, disclosure."[5] While they are different words, they both convey a similar sentiment. John wants to reveal Jesus in all His glory. In John 2:1–11, at the beginning of Jesus' ministry, there is the record of Jesus changing the water to wine. This passage concludes: "This, the first of his signs, Jesus did at Cana in Galilee, and manifested his glory. And his disciples believed in him" (verse 11).

The resurrected Jesus

The final chapter of John's Gospel is the last of the signs to be recorded by John to reveal the glory of the resurrected Jesus. John employs repetition, like many other authors of Scripture, to emphasize an important point. In John 21:1, he repeats, "Jesus revealed himself . . . he [Jesus] revealed himself." Importantly, John repeats this point a third time in this chapter: "Jesus was revealed to the disciples" (verse 14). John wants people to see, hear, experience, and know this resurrected Jesus.

John was at this event by the Sea of Tiberias; he experienced the event. He wants to take his readers to this same place so that each reader can also experience what he experienced that early morning by the Sea of Tiberias with the resurrected Jesus. To ensure that readers recognize John as a trusted and truthful witness, he repeatedly but humbly identifies himself as being present in the following ways:

- "*sons* of Zebedee" (verse 2)
- "*that disciple* whom Jesus loved" (verse 7)
- "Peter turned and saw the disciple whom Jesus loved following them, *the one who also had leaned back against him* during the supper and had said, "*Lord, who is it that is going to betray you*?" (verse 20)
- When Peter saw *him*, he said to Jesus, "Lord, what about this *man*?" (verse 21)
- Jesus said to him, "If it is my will that *he* remain until I come, what is that to you? You follow me!" (verse 22)
- So the saying spread abroad among the brothers that *this disciple was not to die*; yet Jesus did not say to him that he was not to die, but, "If it is my will that *he* remain until I come, what is that to you?" (verse 23)
- *This is the disciple who is bearing witness about these*

things, and who has written these things, and we know that his testimony is true. (verse 24)

- Now there are also many other things that Jesus did. Were every one of them to be written, *I* suppose that the world itself could not contain the books that would be written (verse 25).

In effect, John is making a clear statement to his readers: "I am an eyewitness to these events. I was there, I saw these details, and I heard these conversations. I know what I am writing about, and these things are true and accurate."

When examining John's personal account, it is reasonable to imagine that he and the other disciples are hungry, drained, and frustrated when the first signs of dawn emerge after unsuccessfully fishing in a boat for the night. There is a Stranger on the shore. It is too dark for the disciples to recognize the distant figure, but John reveals to his readers that the Stranger is Jesus. This allows his readers to witness the whole scene as it unfolds—as the Stranger reveals Himself to the disciples. This scene is also reminiscent of John 20:11–18, where Jesus revealed Himself to Mary Magdalene after His resurrection.

Through the early dawn gloom comes a polite inquiry from the Stranger, "Children, do you have any fish?" (John 21:5). With a blend of disappointment and embarrassment, the disciples sheepishly reply, "No." The voice from the shore then says, "Cast the net on the right side of the boat, and you will find some" (verse 6). Without hesitation or argument, they cast the net. The Stranger said they would find "some." In reality, they found more fish than seven men could haul. There is an implied message here for Jesus' disciples of all eras. The promises of God provide us with more than we can imagine and more than we can haul.

It is at this point in the text that John recognizes the unknown Person on the shore as Jesus. It is as though Jesus' miraculously filling an empty fishing net—a net that stubbornly remained empty the whole night despite repeated casts—was the revealing sign of Jesus for John.

John then reveals Jesus to Peter. The spontaneity of Peter's response is what readers have come to know, love, and expect of Peter. "He put on his outer garment, . . . and threw himself into the sea" (verse 7). Such was Peter's desire to be with Jesus. Picturing Peter swimming, splashing, and dashing through the water brings to mind what Peter said to Jesus at the Last Supper. At one point during his conversation with Jesus, Peter wanted not just his feet washed but also his hands and head (John 13:9). It seems as though that wish has become a reality. As John 21 proceeds, readers will have another reason to recall and ponder the Last Supper and another conversation shared between Jesus and Peter.

Breakfast by the sea

As the hungry and fatigued disciples arrive on the shore, Jesus is preparing breakfast for them. John describes the fire. It is not just a nondescript fire; John provides detail. It is a charcoal fire. John outlines the menu and how it is cooked. The fish are laid out on the coals with bread (verse 9). Just a little more evidence that John was there as a participant and as an eyewitness. John also shares other specifics: 153 large fish were caught, and the net was not torn (verse 11).

Jesus invites the disciples, "Come and have breakfast" (verse 12). "Jesus came and took the bread and gave it to them, and so with the fish" (verse 13).

After breakfast, Jesus initiates a conversation. It is a difficult but important conversation. John provides us with the details:

"When they had finished breakfast, Jesus said to Simon Peter . . ." (verse 15). This conversation was in the presence of the disciples. It needed to be. Ellen G. White explains why:

> Another lesson Christ had to give, relating especially to Peter. Peter's denial of his Lord had been in shameful contrast to his former professions of loyalty. He had dishonored Christ, and had incurred the distrust of his brethren. They thought he would not be allowed to take his former position among them, and he himself felt that he had forfeited his trust. Before being called to take up again his apostolic work, he must before them all give evidence of his repentance. Without this, his sin, though repented of, might have destroyed his influence as a minister of Christ. The Saviour gave him opportunity to regain the confidence of his brethren, and, so far as possible, to remove the reproach he had brought upon the gospel.[6]

This open and honest conversation between Jesus and Simon Peter restored Peter and gave him the opportunity to express his genuine love for Jesus three times. But it also revealed a greater love—Jesus' love for Peter and all humanity. Peter, though he failed, was not cast away, jettisoned, never to have a purpose again. No, grace restored Peter. Peter had very significant responsibilities to feed Jesus' lambs, tend Jesus' sheep, and feed Jesus' sheep (verses 15–17).

The people Jesus loves

This concluding chapter of John reveals a risen, victorious Savior who has conquered sin and Satan. His goodness has triumphed over all evil. In victory, He is not arrogant nor is He seeking glory, but He has a very real glory, albeit an unconventional glory.

Jesus is revealed in this final chapter—helping people in their daily lives, filling their nets, cooking for them, seeking their fellowship, restoring them, forgiving them, and loving them. These people are normal people—people who make mistakes and have regrets. These are the people Jesus loves. John, who is profoundly aware of being loved by Jesus and who witnessed all these things, says this is what "the Word [who] became flesh and dwelt among us" looks like (John 1:14). This is what He does. He is full of grace and truth. This is His glory.

John's final appeal to his readers of all eras is to know this Jesus—to experience His grace and truth and live in His love.

---

1. Joan Acocella, "The Terror and the Fascination of Pompeii," Books, *New Yorker*, February 10, 2020, https://www.newyorker.com/magazine/2020/02/17/the-terror-and-the-fascination-of-pompeii.

2. Cynthia Damon, trans., "[Pliny the Younger's] Letters to Tacitus on Vesuvius: Letter 6.20," in Ronald Mellor, *The Historians of Ancient Rome: An Anthology of the Major Writings*, 3rd ed. (New York: Routledge, 2013), 391.

3. Unless otherwise noted, all Scripture quotations in this chapter are from the Holy Bible, English Standard Version®.

4. Walter Bauer, William F. Arndt, F. Wilbur Gingrich, and Frederick W. Danker, *A Greek-English Lexicon of the New Testament and Other Early Christian Literature*, 3rd ed. (Chicago: University of Chicago Press, 2000), s.v. "φανερόω" (*phaneroō*).

5. Bauer, Arndt, Gingrich, and Danker, s.v. "ἀποκάλυψις" (*apokalypsis*).

6. Ellen G. White, *The Desire of Ages* (Mountain View, CA: Pacific Press®, 1940), 811.